# San Francisco

*A Pictorial Celebration*

by Christopher J. Craig

*Photography by Elan Penn*

Sterling Publishing Co., Inc.
New York

Design by Michel Opatowski
Edited by J. E. Sigler
Layout by Gala Pre Press Ltd.

Penn Publishing gratefully acknowledges the following institutions and individuals
for allowing photographs from their collections to be reproduced in this book:

Archbishop's Mansion  56, 57
Carlos Avila Gonzalez/San Francisco Chronicle/Corbis  111
Chicago Daily News negatives collection. Courtesy of the Chicago Historical
Society 8–10
Mark Darley/ © Corporation of the Fine Arts Museums  109
Denver Public Library  12–14
Kevin Fleming/Corbis  28
Library of Congress, Washington, D.C.  16–19
San Francisco Historical Photograph Collection, San Francisco Public Library  20, 21
San Francisco Maritime National Historical Park  99
San Francisco Zoo  146
The San Francisco Fairmont Hotel  48
Joseph Sohm; Visions of America/Corbis 112–113
Wells Fargo Bank, N.A  108
David Wakely  109

**Library of Congress Cataloging-in-Publication Data**

Craig, Christopher J.
San Francisco: a pictorial celebration / by Christopher J. Craig ; photography by Elan Penn.
    p. cm.
Includes index.
ISBN-13: 978-1-4027-2388-9
ISBN-10: 1-4027-2388-1
    1. Historic buildings—California—San Francisco—Pictorial works. 2. Historic sites—
    California—San Francisco—Pictorial works. 3. San Francisco (Calif.)—Pictorial
    works. 4. San Francisco (Calif.)—Buildings, structures, etc.—Pictorial works. 5. San
    Francisco (Calif.)—Description and travel. 6. San Francisco Bay Area (Calif.)—
    Pictorial works. 7. San Francisco Bay Area (Calif.)—Description and travel. I. Penn,
    Elan. II. Title.

F869.S38A2 2006
979.4'6100222—dc22

                                                            2005057552


                        2  4  6  8  10  9  7  5  3  1

Published by Sterling Publishing Co., Inc.
387 Park Avenue South, New York, NY 10016
© 2006 by Penn Publishing Ltd.
Distributed in Canada by Sterling Publishing
c/o Canadian Manda Group, 165 Dufferin Street
Toronto, Ontario, Canada M6K 3H6
Distributed in the United Kingdom by GMC Distribution Services
Castle Place, 166 High Street, Lewes, East Sussex, England BN7 1XU
Distributed in Australia by Capricorn Link (Australia) Pty. Ltd.
P.O. Box 704, Windsor, NSW 2756, Australia

Sterling ISBN-13: 978-1-4027-2388-9
ISBN-10: 1-4027-2388-1

For information about custom editions, special sales, premium and
corporate purchases, please contact Sterling Special Sales
Department at 800-805-5489 or specialsales@sterlingpub.com.

*Opposite: Golden Gate Bridge.*

# Contents

## Oases of Education and Entertainment: Museums, Performing Arts Centers, Cinemas, and Sports Parks . .84

## The Multicultural Metropolis: Unique Neighborhoods, Streets, and Squares . . . . . . . . . . . .114

## What a Beautiful Day! Parks and Recreation . . . . . . . . . . . . .134

# San Francisco: Golden Gateway to the Pacific

There is a multitude of reasons why travel books and magazines continually rate San Francisco among the top ten most desirable destinations in the world. The enchanting sounds of foghorns and cable car bells, invigorating ocean air, mild Mediterranean climate, quirky rollercoaster topography, natural scenic beauty, cultural diversity, and distinctive neighborhoods and landmarks—all contribute to the city's regional charm.

In addition to these endearing features, this national treasure possesses a fascinating history, wrought with as many ups and downs as a ride in the famed cable cars that climb up and down her many hills. Even through extreme periods of boom and bust, glory and ruin, San Francisco's resilience and perseverance have managed to keep her on the track of progress. Vibrant, dynamic, and in a constant state of rebirth and reinvention, it is fitting that the city's flag and official seal both depict a phoenix rising from the ashes.

Spanish exploration of upper California began in the mid-1500s, but it wasn't until 1776 that a Spanish outpost was established in what is now called San Francisco. That era came to an end in 1821, when Mexico won its independence from Spain; four years later, California became part of Mexico. During the 45-year Mexican-Californio period, as it is now called, the population in the San Francisco area grew into a small pueblo at Yerba Buena Cove. That humble town of Yerba Buena became San Francisco after, in 1846,

*Native women watching men play a game at a mission near San Francisco, 1822. The illustration was done by Russian-born artist Louis Choris (1795–1828), made during the Kotzebue Expedition of 1815–16.*

California was taken by the United States in the Mexican-American War. Just two years later, gold was discovered in the Sierra foothills north of San Francisco. Like an explosion, word spread around the globe. Within a single year, the population of the small port city of about 1,000 residents swelled to approximately 25,000; by 1851, one year after California officially became the 31st state in the Union, approximately 500,000 people had already made their way to the "golden" State of California.

## Icons of City Identity:
### Distinguished Historic Landmarks

The Gold Rush not only brought waves of immigration: it transformed the quiet hamlet into the primary commercial and financial capital of the American West. The Old U.S. Mint, at Fifth and Mission Streets, stands today as a symbolic testament to San Francisco's importance in local and national finance and commerce during the later half of the nineteenth century and into the early twentieth century. Likewise, the 1898 Ferry Building, a lovely clock tower and plaza overlooking the east Bay, embodies the city's primary role as a commercial port. As these two grandiose structures testify, the transition from coastal village to major port city did not happen overnight—but it certainly seemed to at the time.

As often befalls "boomtowns," San Francisco experienced more than her fair share of medical epidemics, fires, and other disasters during the uncontrolled growth of the nineteenth and early twentieth centuries. On April 18, 1906, however, all those calamities and disasters past would seem like mere rehearsals for the great tragedy of that dreadful day. In the early morning hours, a major earthquake struck the city with a force unparalleled in modern American history. The quake instantly paralyzed the city, and with its roads and water pipes destroyed, little could be done to fight the raging fires that followed. In a matter of a few days, all San Francisco was leveled to smoldering ruins.

During the next nine years, the city reconstructed itself literally like a phoenix rising from its own ashes. San Francisco City Hall and the Palace of Fine Arts are the two landmarks that best represent the reconstruction effort. Both of the magnificent structures were completed in 1915, the year marking the official end of the Reconstruction Era. The Palace of Fine Arts is what is left of the Panama-Pacific International Exposition of 1915, the spectacular fair that announced to the world that San Francisco was back in business and thriving after the disaster.

Its unique susceptibility to natural disasters—and its proven capacity to overcome them oh-so-gracefully—has earned the great city of commerce another reputation: that of a stalwart metropolis, resilient and enduring in the face of just about anything. Even during the Great Depression, when labor relations were particularly tense, unemployment was high, and Socialism's popularity was on the rise, San Francisco was taking blow after blow—but she would not be knocked down. In spite of and in the midst of it all, the city built the marvelous Golden Gate Bridge and the San Francisco-Oakland Bay Bridge, both financed by the New Deal's Works Progress Administration. The engineering marvels managed not just to boost San Franciscans' morale, but to maintain the city's progress toward the modern commercial metropolis it is today.

By the end of World War II, San Francisco's population rose again to an all-time high of nearly 850,000, spurring another building boom and further urban development and expansion. By this time, the city's urban identity was beginning to congeal into a definite form, and it was, well . . . unusual. Nowadays, underground movements, alternative lifestyles, and general unorthodoxy and unconventionality are as synonymous with San Francisco as cable cars and sourdough bread. It all started with the reign of the revered eccentric Emperor Norton I in the late nineteenth century. Since then San Francisco has been garnering a reputation as a

*Pedestrians walking up Nob Hill past the ruins of buildings toward the Fairmont Hotel after the 1906 earthquake and fire.*

haven for freethinkers. The City Lights Bookstore in the North Beach District continued this tradition when it served as headquarters for many renowned writers associated with the anything-but-mainstream Beat generation of the 1950s. One of the city's most recognizable and symbolic landmarks is a prime symbol of this non-conformist nature: In defiance of the standard box-shaped buildings surrounding it, the enormously tall, pyramid-shaped Transamerica Building is an unignorable fixture of the city skyline.

## Golden Age Relics: Grand Hotels and Homes

Not long after gold was found in California, silver was discovered in mines in Nevada, and the famed Comstock Lode—the largest silver vein deposit ever discovered in America—brought much wealth to many San Franciscans who had financed the mining operation. At about the same time, the railroad was developing into a nationwide industry, and there were plenty of transportation fortunes to be made out in the far-flung reaches of the Wild West. The term Gilded Age is often used to describe this (tax-free) period, when an elite group of American industrialists and businessmen amassed vast fortunes. In San Francisco as elsewhere, the great mansions and estates built by these ridiculously wealthy men are remnants of a bygone era characterized by excess and extravagance.

The "Big Four," a local historical term referring to the nineteenth-century railroad magnates Leland Stanford, Charles Crocker, Mark Hopkins,

*Refugees standing in bread line after the 1906 earthquake and fire.*

and Colis P. Huntington, is also used to describe San Francisco's four historic luxury hotels: the Fairmont, the St. Francis, the Palace, and the Mark Hopkins. Located in the Downtown and Nob Hill Districts, each of the hotels dates back to the early twentieth century and exhibits the stylistic opulence and architectural grandeur associated with the Gilded Age.

Great men do not just build great rooms for their city's guests; they of course live in great homes themselves. San Francisco's residential landmarks cover a variety of architectural styles and number in the hundreds. Best known among these are the Victorian Stick-style and Queen Anne-style dwellings built between 1860 and 1900. The Westerfeld House (circa 1886) is a prime example of the Victorian Stick style, and the Haas-Lilienthal House (circa 1889) is representative of the Queen Anne style. In the first decade of the twentieth century, the city's financial elite began to build in the Gothic Revival, Arts and Crafts, Neo-Georgian, Baroque Revival, and Beaux Arts styles. Prime examples are the French Baroque Revival, white limestone Spreckels Mansion and the Second French Empire-style Archbishop's Mansion. The Beaux Arts style, also called Classical Revival, was usually associated with San Francisco's legacy of grand public buildings, but turn-of-the-century millionaires found the loftiness and grandiosity of the style befitting their social status. Silver mine millionaire James C. Flood, who built his brownstone mansion on Nob Hill, was just one such man.

## Shrines of Awe and Honor: Religious Structures, Memorials, and Monuments

San Francisco has few structures able to compete with those houses of luxury, but if any do pull it off, it's undoubtedly the houses of worship. Least among them in appearance but grandest in historic dignity is Mission Dolores, a small adobe mission church that was one of the first two buildings erected by the area's early Spanish settlers. Completed in 1791, the humble but beautiful building is the city's oldest intact structure, a virtual relic of the past revered for its importance to early San Francisco history and culture.

Today, the city is home to hundreds of religious institutions, with just about as many denominations. Most of these structures exhibit strikingly different architecture from that found in the grand public buildings, hotels, and homes of the same era, having taken their design cues not from Classical styles, but from Medieval European, Eastern, or early American religious structures. Old St. Mary's Cathedral in Chinatown and the First Unitarian Universalist Church of San Francisco are two such examples, both built in the Medieval European Gothic style in the mid- to late nineteenth century. The popularity of this style among the city's religious structures is evident in its continuity: Grace Cathedral, built in 1964, exhibits the same Gothic features as those two churches built a century before her.

All three Gothic edifices are registered as city, state, or national landmarks, or as a combination of the three. That goes as well for the city's more unusual religious structures, including the Swedenborgian Church, a prime example of the early twentieth-century American Arts and Crafts School; Holy Virgin Cathedral, whose glittering gold onion domes are typical of Russian Orthodox ecclesiastical architecture; and the

*Golden Gate Park between 1903 and 1906.*

*View of the Panama-Pacific International Exposition complex of domed buildings, 1915. The Palace of Fine Arts is to the west; Lyon Street, Alcatraz, and Angel Island are also visible. Photographed by George L. Beam.*

sumptuous Temple Emanu-El, a Byzantine-style synagogue so gorgeous that it was designated by the American Institute of Architects as the finest piece of architecture in northern California.

Though San Francisco doesn't have nearly the number of memorials found in older East Coast cities such as Washington, D.C., and Boston, a relatively sizable amount of memorial landmarks can be found around town. Wartime commemorations include the Dewey Monument in Union Square, a tribute to Admiral Dewey and U.S. Naval forces for their gallant 1898 victory over Spanish forces in the Philippines; and the Lone Sailor Memorial, honoring all U.S. Navy, Coast Guard, Marine Corps, and Merchant Marines who passed through the Golden Gate in defense of their country. Many think of San Francisco's strategic location on the bay solely in terms of commercial and trade utility, but both of these memorials testify to the existence of a proud naval heritage here as well.

Several important San Francisco memorials manifest the city's reputation as an international headquarters for such causes as civil rights, human rights, and the promotion of compassion and understanding between individuals and nations. Most notable among these are the Holocaust Memorial Sculpture in Lincoln Park, the National AIDS Memorial Grove in Golden Gate Park, and the Martin Luther King Jr. Memorial in Yerba Buena Gardens. Always on the frontlines of the battle for individual freedom, tolerance, and peace, San Francisco remembers in these memorials those she unfortunately could not save.

Many of the city's greatest memorials and monuments were constructed through philanthropic gifts from prominent individuals and supplemented by city funds. For example, Lotta's Fountain was a gift to the city from the nineteenth-century vaudeville superstar Lotta Crabtree. The nearby Mechanics Monument was a gift from James M. Donahue, given in memory of his father, industrialist Peter Donahue. The Pioneer Monument in Civic Center was created

and installed using funds bequeathed to the city by real estate magnate James Lick. Such generous donations not only beautify the city to the benefit of all: they bind all citizens together in the knowledge that San Francisco has been loved and called home by such diverse benefactors as these. Indeed, Lillie Hitchcock Coit's desire to "add to the beauty of the city I have always loved" gave birth to the city's most famed memorial, Coit Tower.

## Oases of Education and Entertainment: Museums, Performing Arts Centers, Cinemas, and Sports Parks

With all those wealthy denizens about town, it was just a matter of time before they started giving the city more than statues and towers. Institutions dedicated to the study of the arts and sciences began to emerge in the city during the last half of the nineteenth century, when San Francisco was notably focused on establishing itself as a sophisticated metropolis and cultural capital of the West rivaling the great cities of the East Coast. Naturally, a new emphasis on culture and technology brought the local intelligentsia out of the woodwork, and San Francisco became the Pacific mecca for artists, scientists, and thinkers.

Many of the early students at the city's first art school, the California School of Design (later renamed the San Francisco Art Institute), became renowned painters or sculptors. An important development for these San Francisco artists and their audiences was the exciting establishment of the San Francisco Museum of Modern Art (SFMOMA) in 1935. For the first time on the West Coast, SFMOMA gave modern artistic masterworks of the twentieth century a proper venue for enjoyment by the public. The Asian Art Museum, erected in 1966, was the city's next great artistic achievement, and is the largest museum of its kind in the United States.

Since San Francisco has become a center of the technological revolution, it probably comes

as no surprise to most people that it was also the site of the first scientific institution in the American West: the California Academy of Sciences, established in 1853. The academy's public offerings include a natural history museum, aquarium, planetarium, and related natural science exhibits. In the same scientific spirit as the academy—but a tad more fun for little (and big) scientists—the Exploratorium opened in 1969 inside the Palace of Fine Arts. For over thirty years, it has been educating and amusing visitors with hundreds of hands-on exhibits related to science, technology, natural phenomena, and human perception.

What's nice about being a late bloomer in the big national picture is that, unlike cities that got their start during less history-friendly eras, San Francisco was born at a time when people were beginning to understand and

cherish the past. Many East Coast cities have demolished or all but forgotten their earliest treasures, but San Francisco began preserving practically from the start. True, a few historically significant sites were not spared the indignity of demolition, particularly during the '60s and '70s. At the very least, however, some of these sites' legacy has been preserved at the many heritage museums throughout the city. Three such precious collections celebrating the various—sometimes quirky—aspects of the city's unique history include: the Musée Mecanique, the National Maritime Museum, and the Cable Car Museum.

Obviously, San Francisco's reputation as a bastion of culture at the edge of a continent would not be complete if it had only bothered with science and the visual arts. The city makes a point of satisfying all sorts of tastes for beauty

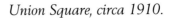
*Union Square, circa 1910.*

and fun, such that the diversity of entertainment here ranges from "high culture" venues like theaters and performing arts centers to more casual, "pop-culture" hangouts like the cinema and ballpark.

Both local and touring plays and musicals can be seen at the Curran, Geary, and Orpheum Theatres, while music and ballet fans flock to the vast San Francisco War Memorial and Performing Arts Center. Those who prefer to spend their evenings in jeans rather than evening gowns head to the Castro Theatre, an opulent movie house that is both architecturally important and revered as San Francisco's last surviving single-screen movie palace. If the Castro's great architecture and classic films are still a little too hoity-toity, shouting and cheering outdoors with hot dogs and beer should fill in the rest of the entertainment gap. San Francisco has two places sports fans can

go wild: SBC Park, the newly built home of the San Francisco Giants, and Candlestick Park, home to the San Francisco '49ers.

### The Multicultural Metropolis: Unique Neighborhoods, Streets, and Squares

As much as people identify San Francisco with her famed cable cars, delicious sourdough bread, and outrageous hills, it's not actually the landmarks, the culture, or even the landscape that makes San Francisco what it is. *San Franciscans* do, and they have come from all over the world, claim all the world's religions, and are famously "worldly" people. It's these people that have given the city her many charming neighborhoods and districts with their unique histories, all reflective of the particular immigrant groups that founded them.

*Right: Rotunda of the Palace of Fine Arts, Panama-Pacific International Exposition, circa 1919. Photographed by J. D. Givens.*

*Below: San Francisco Harbor, circa 1920. Photographed by Wesley W. Swadley.*

North Beach and Fisherman's Wharf, for example, were both predominantly occupied by Italian immigrants in the nineteenth century. North Beach has managed to retain enclaves of traditional Italian businesses, but Fisherman's Wharf, which has become one of the city's top tourist attractions, has lost much of its traditional Italian feel due mainly to overcommercialization. This has been the fate of most of San Francisco's neighborhoods. Multiethnicity and multiculturalism are now the norm. It is not unusual to find a Vietnamese restaurant, a Mexican burrito joint, and an Indian food cafeteria all on the same block. However, some neighborhoods do still exhibit signs of a unique monoethnicity or monoculturalism—at least for a few blocks.

Chinatown is one such neighborhood. Currently home to the second-largest Chinese community in the United States, the small district is a major tourist attraction whose exotic flavor is so condensed that visitors almost feel like they're on a movie set.

Other neighborhood histories are more complex. The Castro District, for example, went from a more or less heterogenous working-class immigrant neighborhood in the nineteenth century to the gay capital of the world in the twentieth. The same political and cultural revolutions of the '60s and '70s that affected that transformation had a similar effect on the Haight-Ashbury District. Beginning as a quiet, middle-class residential neighborhood in the late

1800s, the district became renowned as the epi-center of the hippie movement during the late 1960s. To this day, it remains an enigmatic area where commercialism and counterculturalism collide amid the sounds of clicking tourist cameras, Grateful Dead hits piped out of store-fronts, and the mumblings of homeless youth begging for spare change.

More conventionally historic areas include Union Square and the surrounding downtown shopping district, as well as two of the city-registered historic districts, Jackson Square and Alamo Square. The latter are virtual time cap-sules of commercial and residential buildings which have had many faces since their inception in the earliest days of the city: the Jackson Square

Historic District is a reliquary of structures dating to the Gold Rush Era; the Alamo Square Historic District, a residential neighborhood renowned for its Victorian Era architecture, is home to the famed "Postcard Row," a must-see for any visitor to San Francisco.

## What A Beautiful Day! Parks and Recreation

Visitors to any of the city's neighborhoods will quickly notice two simple facts: San Francisco's unique location offers unequaled natural scenic beauty and breathtaking views, and her many hills provide all the lookout points one could ever desire. Fully conscious of this, the city has reserved

*Joe DiMaggio at Fisherman's Wharf sometime between 1933 and 1937.*

nearly 3,600 acres as parkland and natural open spaces for public use. The over 140 parks and recreation centers in San Francisco vary in size from the largest—Golden Gate Park, at 1,013 acres—to neighborhood parks and gardens offering little more than a small patch of grass and a couple of benches. Among the city's high-altitude vistas are Buena Vista Park and Twin Peaks, both of which offer sweeping panoramic views of the great metropolis and its environs below.

Golden Gate Park is home to some of the city's best scenic treasures, including the Conservatory of Flowers, the tranquil and exotic Japanese Tea Garden, and the lush Botanical Gardens at Strybing Arboretum. Other city parks and recre-

ation centers include Stern Grove, an outdoor concert venue; Ocean Beach and the Great Highway on the Pacific Coast; and of course, the world-renowned San Francisco Zoo.

In addition to city parks, San Francisco is home to one of the most-visited national parks in the country, the Golden Gate National Recreation Area (GGNRA). Created by Congress in 1972, the vast national park lines San Francisco's western and northwestern coastline, and includes the Marin Headlands, San Francisco Maritime National Historic Park, Fort Point and the Presidio, and Alcatraz Island. Of all these marvelous attractions, Alcatraz Island National Historic Park is by far the most renowned (or rather, notorious) and

*Group of people taking a final ride on a cable car before it is taken out of service, December 8th, 1954.*

the most popular with tourists. The National Park Service offers regular tours and has meticulously preserved the island's many historic structures as well as its natural resources.

San Francisco continues to see drastic changes: the sharp rise in homelessness in the 1980s, the 1989 Loma Prieta earthquake, the development of the Internet during the 1990s, and the painful bursting of the dot-com investment bubble at the close of the twentieth century. Nevertheless, the city remains as resilient and optimistic as ever. Highly successful tourist, legal, and financial industries have all but guaranteed San Francisco economic survival, and

the fields of life sciences and biotechnology research seem to promise another gilded age of prosperity soon.

That good fortune shouldn't really come as a surprise. After all, San Francisco may very well be home to more freethinkers and innovators than any other American city. Conservative political commentators regularly label San Francisco as a city on the brink of full-blown depravity because of it, but minds that will not be bound by society's mores are the very same ones that will not be bound by the limitations of the present. Because of them, the future is nearer and brighter than ever before—perhaps that's where this "Golden Gateway" *really* leads.

# Icons of City Identity:
# Distinguished Historic
# Landmarks

# Old U.S. Mint

Looking very much like a weathered ancient Greek temple, the Old U.S. Mint, also known locally as the "Granite Lady," is located just around the corner from the busy Powell and Market Street intersection in the downtown shopping district. The massive structure is significant as one of the finest examples of Greek Revival architecture in the country and as San Francisco's oldest stone building. It is listed in the National Register of Historic Places and has been designated both an official San Francisco Historic Landmark and a California Historic Landmark.

Alfred B. Mullet, Supervising Architect of the Treasury Department from 1866 to 1874, was chosen to design the structure. As the San Francisco Bay Area was already known for its predisposition to seismic activity, Mullet was determined to design the mint to withstand earthquakes. As a result, the "Granite Lady" has a granite basement, and an additional two feet of granite reinforcement were anchored to the foundation with iron rods. Soon before the project's completion, Mullett stated that he would risk his professional reputation on its stability, providing his design plans were carried out to the letter.

His precautions proved to be warranted—and his reputation remained intact—when, in 1906,

*Previous page: Golden Gate Bridge viewed from Marin Headlands.*

the solid structure withstood the great earthquake and fire that devastated most of the city. Valiant firefighters doused the mint with water, and mint employees and volunteers secured the building during the looting that swept the city in the quake's aftermath, thereby saving the $200 million in gold that was housed within. When order had been established, the resilient (albeit charred) stone temple stood alone, surrounded by several blocks of smoldering ruins. After the disaster, the mint became one of the city's primary locations of relief aid, and, since the majority of San Francisco's banking and financial institutions had been completely destroyed, it also played a crucial role in financing the city's reconstruction.

Coining operations resumed soon after 1906. By 1934, the mint housed one-third of the nation's gold supply in its vaults and was a major coin producer for several countries around the world. In 1937, minting operations were moved to another federal mint in San Francisco, and the "Old Mint," as it became known, was turned into federal office space. After a period of vacancy and a stint as a currency museum, ownership of the landmark was transferred to the city of San Francisco, who in turn designated the San Francisco Museum and Historical Society as its "dollar-a-year" lessee. The organization is now in the process of raising funds to turn the Old Mint into a museum of San Francisco history.

# The Ferry Building

For more than a century, this majestic landmark at the foot of Market Street has graced the eastern waterfront and served as a prominent welcome for those arriving in San Francisco by ferry. Completed in 1903, the building replaced the 1875 wooden Ferry House that previously occupied the site. Later, it would become one of the world's busiest transportation terminals. A. Page Brown was chosen to design the new building, but his planning was cut short by his death in 1894, and A. C. Schweinforth assumed responsibility for completion of the architectural design. The Ferry Building's 235-foot clock tower was modeled after the twelfth-century

bell tower of Spain's Cathedral of Seville. The interior nave features ceramic and brick arches and mosaic floors. The entire 660-foot-long steel-framed structure was constructed upon a massive foundation of pine pilings and concrete arches that was once noted as the largest such foundation over water in the world. This foundation has allowed the building to withstand two major earthquakes with relatively minor damage.

Throughout the early twentieth century, the Ferry Building served as the main transportation hub of the city. In time, however, increased automobile use, freeway construction, and the completion of the two bridges that connect the city with its northern and eastern neighbors reduced the bustle on ferries and public transportation. In 1957, the double-decker Embarcadero Freeway was built directly in front of the Ferry Building, obstructing the view of the picturesque landmark for 35 years. After the 1989 Loma Prieta earthquake, the freeway was judged unsafe and torn down—to much local fanfare.

The Ferry Building has recently undergone a major renovation and redevelopment. The expansive nave now houses a marketplace with several upscale specialty food and produce shops on the ground floor, and general office space is leased on the second and third floors. Thoughtful preservation and restoration efforts have returned much of the building's façade and interior public hall to their original splendor.

# James Flood Building

Boldly looming over crowds of bustling shoppers and tourists at the Market and Powell Street cable car terminus, this 12-story Classical Revival office building has been a solid fixture at the intersection for 100 years. Built in 1904, it replaced the Baldwin Theater and Hotel that was destroyed by fire six years earlier.

James C. Flood commissioned the building to honor his father, silver mine magnate James L. Flood, who died in 1889. Architect Albert Bliss designed the monumental steel-framed structure, which, for a time, was the largest building west of the Mississippi. The building survived the 1906 earthquake and fire, but did suffer damage, primarily to the first and second floors, and to sections of the exterior's gray Colusa sandstone facing.

After the building was restored in 1907, the Southern Pacific Railroad occupied most of its available office space until 1917. Hard-boiled crime novelist Dashiell Hammett worked in the building from 1915 to 1921 as an employee of the Pinkerton Detective Agency. Hammett is best known for creating the fictional character Sam Spade, a private eye made famous in *The Maltese Falcon* and his other pulp crime classics. Woolworth's Department Store moved into the first three floors of the building after World War II and stayed until 1996. The old Woolworth's site is currently occupied by the flagship store of San Francisco-based retail clothing giant The Gap.

The building was slated for demolition in 1952 and supposed to be replaced by a more modern structure, but was luckily spared when the federal government requisitioned the site for military use at the beginning of the Korean War. Though in constant use, the building was in major need of an overhaul by the early 1990s, when James Flood, grandson of James C. Flood, spared no expense in restoring the landmark to its original stunning grandeur.

## Ghirardelli Square

Currently a popular shopping and dining complex, this block is formed by some of San Francisco's most cherished landmarks. The first structure to be built on the site was the Pioneer Woolen Mill, founded in 1859. The company was later contracted by the Union Army to manufacture uniforms during the Civil War. In 1893, the building was purchased by confectioner Domingo Ghirardelli, who used it as a manufacturing site for his growing chocolate company.

Ghirardelli had several more buildings constructed on the site in 1915, including the Power House, the Chocolate Factory, the Mustard Building, apartment buildings for factory employees, and, most notably, the handsome Clocktower, which was modeled after the Château de Blois in France. In 1923, two floors were added to the original building—now called the Cocoa Building—to serve as a base for a 15-foot illuminated sign spelling out "Ghirardelli."

The sign has remained a permanent fixture of the waterfront skyline since its construction and is still visible for miles.

The building complex was purchased in the 1950s by William Matson Roth, who later renovated it into a marketplace. Landscape architect Lawrence Halprin and architects Wurster, Bernardi, and Emmons designed the new space: one of the first conversions of its kind in the nation. The site opened to the public with the new name of Ghirardelli Square in 1964.

The square was designated an official city landmark in 1965. Ghirardelli Chocolate production facilities were moved soon thereafter to nearby San Leandro, California. In 1998, the European confection giant Lindt and Sprungli acquired Ghirardelli Chocolate Company—but the delicious chocolate invented by Domingo Ghirardelli in the 1800s is still enjoyed by millions worldwide.

# Sentinel Building

Located at the corner of Columbus Avenue and Kearny Street, this late Victorian steel-framed building marks the intersections of North Beach, Chinatown, Jackson Square, and downtown. The building features a copper dome and a flatiron exterior that has oxidized, giving the building its signature blue-green color.

The structure was designed by architects Salfield and Kohlberg. It was under construction when the 1906 earthquake struck, but suffered no damage and opened on schedule the following year. Political kingpin Abraham "Boss" Reuf helped finance the costly construction, and years later—after serving time in San Quentin State Prison for graft charges—located his office on the top floor.

A prized restaurant named Caesar's was located in the building during the 1920s, and is credited with creating the popular salad that bears the name to this day. The restaurant was later closed for liquor law violations during Prohibition. In the 1940s and '50s, the building fell into decay, but in 1958 it was purchased and restored by local businessman Rob Moor. Moor renamed the building Columbus Tower and sold it to the popular singing group the Kingston Trio a year later. The trio had made their debut in the Hungry i, a nightspot located in the building's basement. In the early 1970s, they sold the building to Academy Award-winning director Francis Ford Coppola, who reinstated the original name of Sentinel Building. Coppola continues to own the landmark, which houses the headquarters of his American Zoetrope Studios and rentable office space. The ground floor of the building is home to the Café Neibaum-Coppola, a bistro associated with his successful winery in Napa, California.

*San Francisco's almost aquatic-looking version of New York's Flatiron Building gets its color from oxidation of its steel façade.*

## San Francisco City Hall

This magnificent civic building is the crown jewel of the Civic Center Historic District. In 1978, the American Institute of Architects declared it one of the finest examples of French Renaissance architecture in the nation. Acclaimed architect Arthur Brown Jr. designed the grand structure in the Beaux Arts style, with heavy use of ornament and stylistic detailing on both the interior and exterior. Brown found much of his inspiration for the design in the dome of the church at Les Invalides in Paris, and the City Hall dome that resulted is notable for being the fifth largest dome in the world, surpassing the height of the United States Capitol by fourteen inches. The $3,499,262 building was officially dedicated on December 28, 1915. After considerable damage caused by the 1989 Loma Prieta earthquake, the building underwent major seismic retrofitting in the 1990s. It now sits not on solid foundation, but on an elaborate system of rubber isolators.

Many newsworthy events have occurred at City Hall over the years. In 1923, President Warren G. Harding died of pneumonia while staying at the Palace Hotel on Market Street. His body lay in state in the opulent City Hall rotunda, as did the body of "Sunny Jim" Rolph when he died in office as governor of California in 1934. Happier news came from City Hall in 1954, when local baseball hero Joe DiMaggio married film actress Marilyn Monroe there.

The most notorious event in the building's history occurred on November 27, 1978, when Mayor George Moscone and the city's first openly gay district supervisor, Harvey Milk, were assassinated there by a deranged, ultra-conservative former district supervisor named Dan White. White had resigned his elected post on San Francisco's Board of Supervisors seventeen days prior to the double murder. During his trial, White's defense team successfully convinced the jury that the former supervisor was under a considerable amount of stress, and that his over-consumption of sweets (particularly "Hostess Twinkies," a cream-filled American favorite) led him over the edge into temporary insanity. The infamous "Twinkie Defense" outraged many local San Franciscans who had been following the trial all year, most notably the gay community. On May 21, when Dan White was sentenced to only seven years for the crime, the verdict sparked the "White Night Riots" later that evening in front of and surrounding City Hall. The Civic Center area suffered some property damage, police cars were set on fire, and there were over a dozen arrests.

In 2004, Mayor Gavin Newsom took a bold and controversial step that made national headlines: he gave the green light for San Francisco City Hall to issue marriage licenses to gay couples, claiming that the California constitution's nonrecognition of such unions was discriminatory. The State of California later put a stop to the marriage license issuances and the matter is currently in the courts.

# Palace of Fine Arts

After the devastating earthquake and fire of 1906, many temporary palaces and pavilions were constructed for the Panama-Pacific International Exposition of 1915 to show the world that San Francisco was back in business and thriving. The fair celebrated the completion of the Panama Canal as well as the four-hundredth anniversary of Balboa's discovery of the Pacific Ocean. The captivating Palace of Fine Arts is the only reminder of that once-glittering world fair.

The buildings for the Panama-Pacific International Exposition were not intended to be permanent. They were made of wooden frames that were covered with burlap fiber and plaster so that they could be easily demolished after the fair. The fine arts building was designed by the prominent Berkeley-based architect Bernard

Maybeck, but many of the decorative elements are credited to William Merchant, an architect at Maybeck's firm.

Opening to phenomenal success on February 20, 1915, the Panama-Pacific International Exposition was like nothing anyone had ever seen before. Three years of effort and $15 million was spent on the exposition that San Francisco Mayor James "Sunny Jim" Rolph described as "the world's wonderland, a carnival of all nations, the playground of the universe." Taking up 635 acres of what is now the Marina District, the exposition grounds were filled with hundreds of buildings, landscaped gardens, statues, fountains, and attractions. Esteemed architects, engineers, designers, and artists from around the country were asked to participate. George W. Kelham, known for his design of the Palace Hotel, was appointed chief of architecture for the fair, and General Electric engineer W. D'Arcy Ryan, known later as the "Aladdin of the 1915 City Luminous," was appointed to design the exposition's elaborate lighting scheme.

The centerpiece of the exposition was the stunning Tower of Jewels, a 43-story Italianate structure that was covered with more than 100,000 dangling colored glass jewels set against miniature mirrors. At night, strategically placed spotlights illuminated the lavish tower, creating a magnificent shimmering effect. Surrounding the tower were fantastic exhibition palaces, all monumental in size, such as the Palace of Machinery, the Festival Hall, the Palace of Fine Arts, and the Palace of Horticulture, which featured a glass dome that surpassed the size of St. Peter's Basilica in Rome. The fair also offered a very popular amusement park area called the Zone, as well as a large area for exhibition buildings of participating states and countries.

When the magical fair's 288-day engagement sadly came to an end on December 4, 1915, demolition began almost immediately. Plans had been made to save the Palace of Fine Arts two months earlier, when a Fine Arts Preservation Day petition garnered 33,000 signatures and

$350,000 for the structure's replication using permanent, durable building materials. As a result, the building was not demolished, but the replication was not to happen for another fifty years. Philanthropist Walter S. Johnson is credited with providing the majority of the financing needed for reconstruction of the site. Molds were carefully made of all the buildings' decorative elements, and the main rotunda and colonnade were reproduced using concrete castings. The majority of the project was completed in 1967.

Today, the rebuilt Palace of Fine Arts is an almost exact replica of the stunning original that inspired it. Surrounded by a swan pond and lush gardens, the cherished landmark has become a fixture of the Marina District, a favorite spot for joggers, bicyclists, and nature lovers. Currently, the gallery area houses a popular science museum called the Exploratorium, which has been operating at the site since 1969. Another of the landmark's best-loved attractions is a 1,000-seat theater, operated by the Palace of Fine Arts League, Inc.

## Hallidie Building

Located in the city's Financial District at 130 Sutter Street, this early Modern structure is notable for being the first glass-curtain-walled building in the world, and it is listed on the National Register of Historic Places. Acclaimed architect Willis Polk designed the eight-story steel-framed building, which was completed in 1918. The all-glass façade is accented with Gothic cast-iron detailing.

Displayed in the lobby of the building is a plaque commemorating the achievements of inventor Andrew Hallidie (1836–1900). Hallidie became quite wealthy for his patent on the manufacturing of wire cables, which were used in cable rail systems worldwide. He is also credited with creating the first cable line in the world, the Clay Street Hill Railroad.

Aside from being a crucial figure in the development of San Francisco's cable car rail system, Hallidie was twice a member of the board of freeholders chosen to form the city charter. Hallidie was a noted advocate of advanced education and served as chairman of the Finance Committee for the University of California for 26 years. He served on the first Board of Trustees of the San Francisco Free Library in 1878, and was also a founding member of the Mechanic's Institute as well as its president from 1868 to 1878.

# City Lights Bookstore

This literary landmark is distinguished as being the first all-paperback bookstore in the United States. It has expanded several times since its opening in 1953, and now houses three floors of new-release and hard-to-find specialty paperbacks and hardbacks.

Founded by poet Lawrence Ferlinghetti and his business partner, Peter D. Martin, City Lights is an independent bookseller and, since 1955, also a publisher of its own line of titles. Although it is best known for its Pocket Poets series, City Lights Publishers now boasts over one hundred titles in print, with at least a dozen or so new works published annually.

The renowned North Beach bookstore was a popular meeting place for poets and authors associated with the "Beat" generation during the late 1950s and early '60s.

The store proudly launched and marketed the controversial works of progressive and avant-garde authors such as Frank O'Hara, Robert Bly, Kenneth Rexroth, and Allen Ginsberg. Ginsberg's *Howl*, published in 1956, caused the arrest of owner Ferlinghetti and bookstore manager Shigeyoshi Murao for the publication and sale of "obscene materials." However, the two won the ensuing court case and were later released, and their well-publicized legal battle became a landmark in the struggle against literary censorship in America.

For nearly 50 years, City Lights has carried on in the spirit of that event. The company is known for its specialization in publishing and selling works of a progressive nature, and has vehemently and publicly opposed literary censorship and cultural conservatism.

# San Francisco-Oakland Bay Bridge

When boomtown San Francisco's mad Emperor Norton I made an imperial decree in 1872 that a bridge and tunnel connecting San Francisco to Oakland should be built, locals rolled their eyes at yet another one of the local eccentric's absurdly grandiose proclamations. Sixty-one years later, however, in the middle of the Great Depression, the revered monarch's vision was realized by the construction of the San Francisco-Oakland Bay Bridge.

Construction was spearheaded by Charles H. Purcell, an accomplished highway engineer and bridge designer who was appointed Chief Engineer of the Bay Bridge in 1931. The bridge was completed six months sooner than the Golden Gate Bridge, which also opened in 1936. Costing upwards of $77 million to construct, it was deemed the most expensive and longest bridge in the world at the time of its completion. The project employed over 6,500 workers, two dozen of whom lost their lives building this engineering marvel, called by President Herbert Hoover "the greatest bridge ever erected by the human race."

The San Francisco-Oakland Bay Bridge is actually three bridges and a tunnel. One suspension bridge crosses from San Francisco to a massive concrete anchorage in the middle of the bay, and from there another suspension bridge continues to Yerba Buena Island. A tunnel runs through the entire island, then a final span connects Yerba Buena Island with the Oakland shore. When built, Yerba Buena Island Tunnel was the biggest single-bore tunnel in the world. The enormous amount of dirt and rocks excavated from the tunnel was used as landfill for the creation of adjacent Treasure Island, site of the 1939–40 World's Fair.

Part of the eastern portion of the bridge collapsed during the 1989 Loma Prieta earthquake. It was repaired relatively quickly, but plans are underway to completely replace the entire eastern span. The western span has already undergone comprehensive seismic retrofitting.

# Golden Gate Bridge

A masterpiece of aesthetic beauty and structural engineering, this 1.22-mile-long suspension bridge is one of the most widely recognized symbols of San Francisco. The registered California Historic Landmark was declared one of the modern Seven Wonders of the World by the American Society of Civil Engineers. Its name is derived from the Golden Gate Strait, which it crosses to connect the northern tip of the San Francisco peninsula with the Marin County headlands facing south.

Railroad tycoon Charles Crocker first posed the idea of a bridge spanning the length of the Golden Gate in 1872, but it wasn't until 1923 that the Association of Bridging the Gate was formed and began leading the efforts to actually establish the bridge. In 1929, the association appointed Joseph Strauss, an accomplished engineer with over 400 drawbridges to his credit, as chief engineer of the project. Strauss brought on board architect Irving Morrow, who is credited with the bridge's Art Deco design elements that are today considered prime examples of the style. The bridge's "International Orange" color is also credited to Morrow, who felt the color would stand out beautifully against the blues and greens of the natural surroundings.

Construction of the bridge commenced on January 5, 1933, under the control of the Works Progress Administration, a federally funded relief program that sponsored scores of public works projects during the Great Depression. Thanks to that program, hundreds of Bay Area construction workers could be hired, sparing them the humiliation of the soup line. On the job, however, they faced major safety concerns, namely the bridge's dizzying height and the often-rough coastal weather. Strauss's main focus was on the safety of these workers, who, although gratefully employed, nevertheless put their lives at risk every day. Strauss insisted that the men wear hardhats—the first time this was ever required on a construction site. Glare-free goggles were also provided, along with face cream to protect against the elements, and dietary advice was given in order to prevent dizziness and vertigo. Strauss even required that a safety net be stretched along the bottom of the entire length of the bridge: a provision that saved the lives of 19 workmen, who became known as the "Half-Way-to-Hell-Club." In spite of all the precautions, ten men still perished on February 17, 1937, when a scaffold holding twelve men fell and ripped through the safety net.

Three months later, on May 27, the bridge was completed, and pedestrians flocked to the majestic site in droves, eager to be among the first to cross what was then the longest suspension bridge in the world. The following day, the bridge opened to motor vehicles, and a steady stream of traffic has been flowing under the two 746-foot towers ever since.

Navigational beacons and warning lights placed on top of the two towers serve as guides for ships and aircraft. Foghorns placed at the bridge's south pier and mid-span have continued to warn maritime vessels—and charm local San Franciscans—since the 1930s. Tolls have increased with time and inflation, and numerous improvements have been made to the landmark over the years. In fact, the bridge requires constant maintenance: currently, it is undergoing several phases of seismic retrofitting.

*Each suspension cable section of the bridge, like the one shown here, contains 27,572 wires.*

# *Transamerica Pyramid*

Recognized worldwide as an icon of San Francisco, this unique architectural marvel has graced the city's skyline since 1972. The modern, 853-foot-high skyscraper is the tallest building in northern California, and its base occupies one full city block. The building's 48 stories are constructed of concrete, glass, steel, and aluminum, and feature a total of 3,678 windows and 18 elevators.

The building's designer, Los Angeles-based architect William Pereira, considered the massive shadows cast by a typical block-style building to be an environmental concern. In order to provide much-needed light to the streets below, he gave the Transamerica Pyramid its innovative shape. The four-sided tapered pyramid shape also offers more stability than a traditional box-style structure: an important feature in earthquake-prone San Francisco.

The building was constructed as the headquarters of the Transamerica Corporation. They have since moved their headquarters, but still retain a small presence in the building and continue to use the image of the structure as their official trademark and logo. Currently, the high-rise provides retail and office space to more than 50 businesses.

The building sits upon the site of what was once known as the Montgomery Block, a haven for artistic and literary figures of the late nineteenth century such as Mark Twain, Robert Louis Stevenson, and Rudyard Kipling, all of whom had offices there.

Due to heightened security concerns, the Transamerica Pyramid is now closed to the general public. There is, however, a virtual observation deck located at street level that provides views from the top of the structure via live video cameras.

*Previous page: Golden Gate Bridge viewed from Presidio Yacht Club.*

Golden Age Relics:
Grand Hotels and Homes

# Fairmont Hotel

Monumental in scale and lavish in design, the Fairmont's architectural grandeur is in keeping with that of its Nob Hill neighbors, the Flood Mansion and the Mark Hopkins Hotel. The hotel was commissioned as a monument to silver mine magnate James G. "Bonanza Jim" Fair by his two daughters in 1902. Since they sold the hotel just two weeks before the 1906 earthquake and fire, the hotel has changed hands—and faces—many times.

The 1906 disaster destroyed all but one of Nob Hill's famed Gilded Age estates. Luckily for the new owners, the Law Brothers, the Fairmont was only moderately damaged. The brothers wisely chose the young local architect Julia Morgan to take charge of the redesign, restoration, and repairs of the hotel. In 1907, the Fairmont assumed its place as a world-class gem when it opened to much fanfare, a fireworks display, and a banquet. The hotel has recently been restored back to Morgan's original 1907 design, revealing original marble floors and gold-trimmed Corinthian columns. All 591 rooms have been refurbished, including the famous 1926 Penthouse, decorated in an "Arabian Nights" theme with a two-story library and rotunda featuring paintings of the nighttime constellations.

The Fairmont's historic Cirque Room, the first bar in town to open after Prohibition, closed some years ago, and the opulent Venetian Room where Tony Bennett first sang "I Left My Heart in San Francisco" is no longer a public room. The Tonga Room, however, a Tiki-style lounge with indoor lake, periodic rainstorms, and renowned tropical drinks, is a local institution and continues to charm both San Franciscans and tourists.

One of the hotel's greatest claims to fame is that, at the end of World War II, it served as a meeting place for the framers of the Charter of the United Nations. Today, it still draws presidents, heads of state, ambassadors, kings, queens, and a host of celebrities through its elegant porte cochere. Along with the St. Francis Hotel, the Palace Hotel, and the Mark Hopkins Hotel, the Fairmont is currently counted as one of the "Big Four" luxury hotels in the city, all of which are designated as historic landmarks.

*Penthouse balcony and view.*

# St. Francis Hotel

Overlooking Union Square for over 100 years, the St. Francis Hotel is a local treasure and one of the "Big Four" historic luxury hotels in San Francisco. Soon after its 1904 opening, the St. Francis garnered a reputation for first-class service. Just how luxurious was it? The hotel employed someone full-time to clean the hotel coinage on a daily basis so that guests would not have to endure dirty currency!

Long a favorite spot for notables, dignitaries, and celebrities, the hotel became the scene of a sensationalized murder scandal in the roaring '20s. After a wild late night party, a female guest was found dead in a suite adjoining that of comedian Roscoe "Fatty" Arbuckle, then the highest-paid silent film star in Hollywood. Fatty found himself embroiled in a murder case that made headlines for months. He was later acquitted of the crime, but the bad media publicity ended his career.

The hotel underwent a complete restoration in time for its one-hundredth anniversary in 2004. Many locals objected to one particular design decision in the otherwise beautifully remodeled lobby: the handsome 1906 Magneto clock that had graced the lobby for almost a century was moved to the back of the hotel's mezzanine. The clock had become a landmark in its own right as a recognizable rendezvous spot; locals knew that "Meet me under the clock" meant "I'll see you in the lobby of the St. Francis Hotel." Preservationists continue to insist that the hotel put the clock back in its traditional spot.

## Palace Hotel

Bank of California cofounder William Ralston's vision of a grand hotel in San Francisco was realized when the first Palace Hotel opened in 1875. Modeled after the great hotels of Europe, the Palace was the first hotel of its kind in the West. The construction costs—an outrageous $5 million—nearly bankrupted Ralston. Unfortunately, he did not even live to see the grand opening: shortly after a financial panic (a common occurrence during the boom and bust era of the early West) caused the closure of the Bank of California, Ralston was found floating in the San Francisco Bay. Apparently, he had suffered a stroke while taking his daily swim. Still, his losses were not yet counted: the glorious hotel he had poured so much money into would burn to the ground in the great 1906 earthquake and fire.

The present structure, opened in 1909, was financed by Ralston's business partner, Senator William Sharon, and designed by architect George Kelham with the East Coast firm of Trowbridge and Livingston. Kelham's design of the hotel's grand interior Garden Court is considered a local masterpiece, and is often used for upscale brunches, banquets, concerts, and special events. Seating over one thousand, the three-story marble-columned room is topped with an elegantly designed stained-glass dome ceiling and several large Austrian crystal chandeliers. The hotel's bar features a beautifully painted mural entitled *The Pied Piper of Hamlin* by renowned American illustrator Maxfield Parrish, which was commissioned for the Palace's 1909 reopening.

The Palace was closed briefly for reparative work between 1989 and 1991. Since its reopening, the magnificent, completely restored hotel has been stunning visitors without interruption.

# Mark Hopkins Hotel

Known locally as one of the "Big Four" historic luxury hotels in San Francisco, the towering hostelry located at 1 Nob Hill has been in operation since its opening in 1926. Local architects Peter Weeks and William Day designed the structure, which appropriates French chateau- and Spanish Renaissance-style architectural elements. Surrounded by enormous panes of glass on the top floor is the hotel's famed cocktail lounge, The Top of the Mark, beloved for its commanding views of the city and San Francisco Bay. The original lounge interior was designed by Castro Theatre architect Timothy Pflueger, but the room has since been remodeled.

During the 1940s, the hotel was host to several historic meetings that contributed to the founding of the United Nations. In 1962, the hotel's original owner, mining engineer and hotel investor George D. Smith, sold the Mark Hopkins to local financier Louis Lurie. Eleven years later, Lurie's heirs established a long-term management contract with the Inter-Continental Hotels Corporation, which continues management operations today.

The hotel stands on the site of the original Mark Hopkins mansion, an elaborate, 40-room, Gothic-style residence that was built in 1878 but sadly destroyed by the famed earthquake and fire of 1906. Hopkins was a founder of the Central Pacific Railroad and shared Nob Hill with San Francisco's wealthy elite, including James Flood, Leland Stanford, and Collis P. Huntington. All four men occupied palatial mansions on the hill during the city's Gilded Age. Today, the Flood Mansion, located directly across the street from the Mark Hopkins Hotel, is the only 1906 survivor of the bunch.

## Westerfeld House

Although it is only one of many treasured Victorian homes located in the Alamo Square Historic District, the Westerfeld House is probably the most well known. The Stick-style Italianate redwood mansion was built in 1889 by German-born architect Henry Geilfuss as a home for William Westerfeld, a successful baker, confectioner, and caterer.

After Westerfeld's death in 1895, the home was sold to Irish-born contractor Jonathan J. Mahoney, a gregarious man who enjoyed entertaining celebrities of the day in the house's 26 rooms. It is said that he hosted radio pioneer Guglielmo Marconi, who supposedly used the tower room to transmit the first radio signals on the West Coast. Famed escape artist and paranormal researcher Harry Houdini is also said to have used the tower room for an experiment sending telepathic messages to his wife across the San Francisco Bay.

Since those exciting experiments, the home has continued to see all sorts of action. A group of Russian émigrés used it as a private club. Several great musicians, including jazz greats John Handy Sr. and Art Lewis, resided there while it was a boardinghouse. And when hippies turned it into a sort of flophouse, gay underground filmmaker Kenneth Anger briefly resided there with his entourage. That bunch included actor Bobby Beausolie, who later joined up with the Charlie Manson cult and currently is serving time in prison for first-degree murder.

After a desperately needed restoration, the Westerfeld Mansion was sold in 1968, and has since served on and off as a bed and breakfast and private residence. The current owners occasionally welcome visitors on organized home tour events sponsored by the San Francisco Historical Society and the Alamo Square Neighborhood Association.

# The James C. Flood Mansion

Originally the private residence of James C. Flood, one of the Nevada Comstock silver mine magnates, this mansion was sold to the Pacific Union Club in 1907 and remains in their possession today. When architect Augustus Laver completed the 42-room home in 1886, it became the first brownstone west of the Mississippi. The expensive reddish brown sandstone was quarried in Connecticut, cut and dressed in New Jersey, and then shipped to San Francisco via the treacherous Cape Horn route. The home cost $1.5 million to construct, including a $30,000 bronze fence that was polished daily by Flood's servants.

Flood's estate was the only one of Nob Hill's renowned Gilded Age mansions to survive the 1906 earthquake and fire. The lavish homes of his neighbors were all constructed of wood and burned to the ground. Flood's mansion didn't stand entirely lonely, at least: the new Fairmont Hotel across the street, constructed of solid stone, also survived the disaster with moderate damage.

Although it is said that the Flood mansion survived the 1906 disaster, it did not survive unscathed: the shell of the home remained intact, but the interior was completely gutted. After the Pacific Union Club took ownership of the estate in 1907, the services of local architect Willis Polk were retained to repair and redesign the house. He altered the top floor and added semicircular wings, giving the building a more Neoclassical appearance. The site was added to the National Register of Historic Places in 1966. Today, the Pacific Union Club continues to use the house as a private meeting place, and so it is not open for public tours.

# Haas-Lilienthal House

Long considered the definitive example of Queen Anne-style Victorian design, the Haas-Lilienthal House has been reviewed in countless architectural magazines and journals. The elegant three-story mansion displays all the common features associated with the style, including gingerbread ornamentation, a cylindrical corner turret, and wooden gables. The interior displays all the trimmings of a proper Victorian upper-class residence, such as embossed wallpapers, marble fireplaces, and an ornately carved oak grand staircase.

Designed by architect Peter R. Schmidt, the house was completed in 1886 as a private residence for wholesale grocer and prominent businessman William Haas and his family. It was an extremely expensive piece of property at the time, costing $18,000 to build. William Haas's daughter Alice and her husband, Samuel Lilienthal, owned and lived in the mansion after 1917, and the home remained in the Haas-Lilienthal family until 1972, when they donated it to the Foundation for San Francisco's Architectural Heritage.

The mansion was added to the National Register of Historic Places in 1979. The Haas-Lilienthal House and the McElroy Octagon House are the only two museum-houses operating in San Francisco. The Haas-Lilienthal House's meticulous preservation and authentic period interiors draw over 6,500 visitors a year.

## Spreckels Mansion

This 55-room, white limestone, Beaux Arts mansion in Pacific Heights was once the home of the beloved local philanthropist Alma Spreckels. Mrs. Spreckels was the wife of Adolph Spreckels, an heir to the Claus Spreckels sugar fortune—hence the popular local nickname for the house, "the Sugar Palace."

The mansion was designed by architects George Applegarth and Kenneth MacDonald Jr., and construction was completed in 1913. Space constraints became an issue during design of the estate, and two nearby homes had to be purchased and subsequently torn down to make room for the Spreckels' five-limousine garage and massive backyard with sweeping views of the San Francisco Bay. Alma Spreckels was an impassioned Francophile and so was quite pleased with the grand French Baroque exterior of the home,

as well as with the interior's spacious Louis XVI ballroom, where she kept her priceless collection of original Rodin sculptures. Indeed, she was so pleased that she later commissioned Applegarth to design the Palace of the Legion of Honor, a monumental art gallery in Lincoln Park financed by the Spreckels family and given as a gift to the city in 1924. Adolph Spreckels died six months prior to the opening of the new museum. Alma Spreckels died 44 years later.

The legacy of Alma's generosity lives on even today. She stands memorialized in bronze, high above the Dewey Monument in Union Square, and her grand museum in Lincoln Park remains a cherished gem of San Francisco's cultural heritage. Her home remains a private residence, now owned by best-selling author Danielle Steele. It is not open for public tours.

*Dining room.*

## Archbishop's Mansion

This Alamo Square mansion was built in 1904 as the official residence of San Francisco's second Catholic Archbishop, Patrick Riordan, but it also served until 1945 as home for his two successors, Archbishops Edward Hanna and John Mitty. All three men were instrumental in building churches, hospitals, and schools throughout the Bay Area during their tenures, and are recognized for their dedicated service to the city and the archdiocese.

The stately mansion was designed in the Second French Empire style by architect Frank Shea, who gave the home its stunning stained glass atrium and mahogany grand staircase. The concrete and reinforced steel foundation is credited with helping the building withstand the 1906 earthquake with minimal structural damage. In the aftermath of that disaster, the mansion served as a refugee center for hundreds of homeless city residents who flocked to high ground at Alamo Square.

Shortly thereafter, the mansion served as home to the Sisters of the Presentation, whose convent on Powell Street had been destroyed. The archdiocese converted the mansion into a Catholic boys' orphanage in 1945, then sold the house in 1972 to a medical center that used the home as a drug rehabilitation program facility. After being sold again in 1980, the house was renovated and reopened in 1983 as a bed and breakfast inn.

*Archbishop's
Mansion parlor.*

# Abner Phelps House

This house is revered as San Francisco's oldest surviving private residence. The consensus among architectural historians is that this structure dates to 1850 and was probably constructed from a carpenter's plan book. The modest building displays subdued Gothic Revival and Colonial features. Little is known for certain about the house, but historians are sure that it was originally built as a farmhouse for lawyer and real estate developer Abner Phelps.

One of many early account relates that the house was prefabricated in Maine and shipped to San Francisco as a build-it-yourself home. Another oral history relates that the house originated in New Orleans, but was dismantled, shipped in sections, and reassembled in San Francisco at the bequest of Abner Phelps' great-granddaughter, who could not bear to leave her Louisiana home behind. Both of these stories were later discredited during restoration, when research proved that the structure is made of California redwood.

The Abner Phelps House is presently located at 1111 Oak Street, but the building has been physically moved around on the lot three times. Construction on Divisadero Street, the home's original address, necessitated the first relocation in the 1890s. Later commercial property development on Divisadero led to a second move to the back of the lot in the 1890s. The structure was later turned 180 degrees to allow for a front yard, thus changing the home's address to Oak Street. The building is currently a private residence and is not open to visitors.

*McElroy Octagon House*

Octagon house architecture was first promoted in America with the 1848 publication of Orson Squire Fowler's *A Home for All*. Fowler was an advocate of healthy living, and he deemed his eight-sided house design most appropriate for human dwelling because it allowed more direct sunlight into each room than a traditional four-sided structure. During the 1850s and '60s, octagon houses began to spring up throughout the United States. San Francisco is said to have possessed five such structures, but today only two remain.

The eight-room McElroy Octagon House was built by miller William C. McElroy in 1861. The home changed hands many times and was vacant and in a state of disrepair when the California branch of the Colonial Dames of America acquired it in 1951. This organization raised the money to relocate the house to the opposite side of Gough Street, where it was completely restored by Warren Perry, Dean of the University of California Berkeley School of Architecture. The home was designated an official city landmark in 1968 and was added to the National Register of Historic Places four years later. Operating as one of only two house-museums in San Francisco, the McElroy Octagon House features interiors and furnishings designed in the Colonial and Federal periods and is open to visitors.

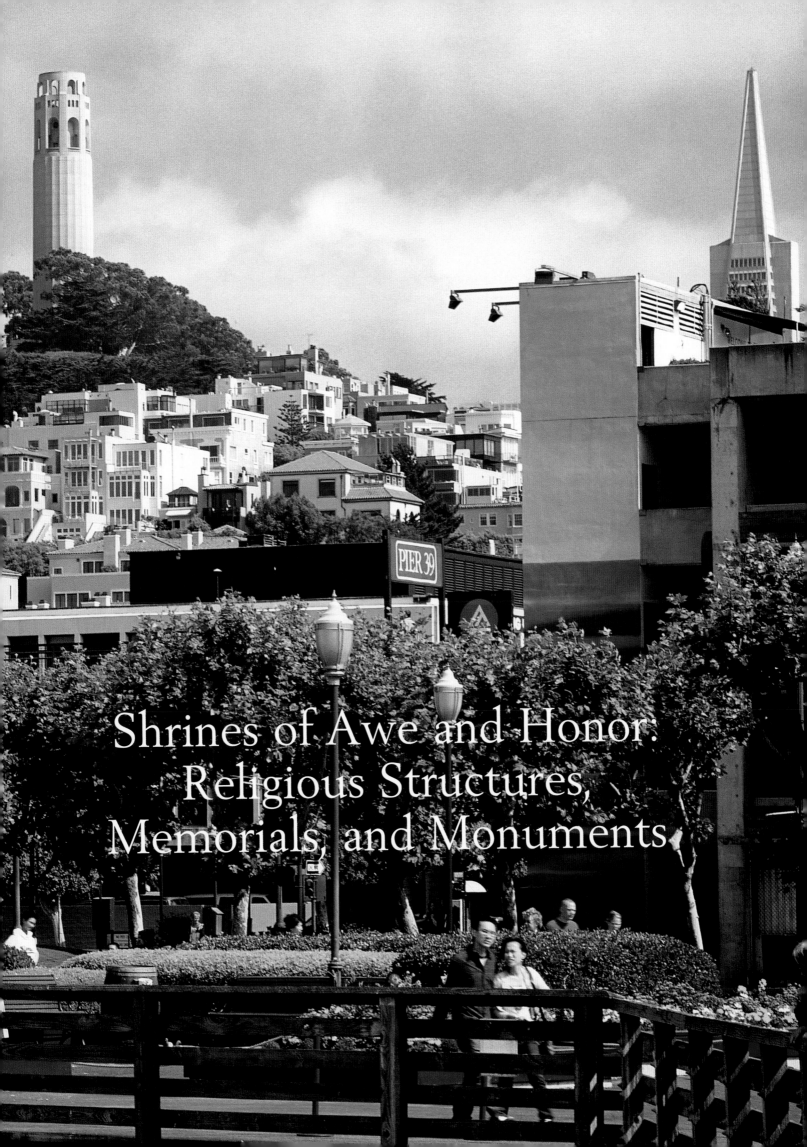

Shrines of Awe and Honor:
Religious Structures,
Memorials, and Monuments

# Mission Dolores (La Misión San Francisco de Asís)

Mission Dolores is San Francisco's most treasured historical landmark and the city's oldest existing structure. It was the sixth in a chain of Spanish Franciscan missions established between 1769 and 1823 along the California coast. Father Francisco Palóu founded *La Misión San Francisco de Asís* on October 9, 1776. Seven months earlier, a scouting party of Spaniards named the nearby inlet *Arroyo de Nuestra Señora de los Dolores*, Lake of Our Lady of Sorrows, which gave rise to the mission's popular name, Mission Dolores.

The church that stands today was erected between 1782 and 1791. Padre Palóu designed the structure, and newly converted Christian Native Americans built it. The walls were made of 4-foot-thick adobe bricks; the floor was constructed of wood, tile, burned brick, and clay; and the ceiling was constructed of wood planks and beams hand-painted with local native designs and held together by hardwood pegs. The mission cemetery's gravestones and markers give testament to the many Native Americans, Spanish, Mexican, and American settlers who died during San Francisco's infancy.

Because the Franciscan missions of California primarily aimed to introduce Catholicism and Spanish culture to local Native Americans, they were not always looked upon with favor by the native peoples of the area. After several missions were burned down by flaming arrows, red tile roofing became a common feature of missions throughout California due to their fire resistance. The handmade red tile roofing at Mission Dolores was added as a precautionary measure in 1794/95.

Mission Dolores is visited by hundreds of tourists daily and includes a gift shop and small museum. Distinguished residents and dignitaries who are fortunate enough to become recipients of the "Key to the City" are told that it was modeled on the key to Mission Dolores and will actually unlock its wooden front doors.

*Previous page: View of Coit Memorial Tower from Fisherman's Wharf.*

# Old St. Mary's Cathedral of the Immaculate Conception

This Gothic red-brick structure, California's first cathedral, was completed in 1854 at the corner of California and Dupont (now Grant) Streets, in the heart of what is now Chinatown. The cathedral was commissioned by San Francisco's first archbishop, Joseph Sadoc Alemany, and designed by architects William Craine and Thomas England. It is constructed of red bricks from New England and has a granite foundation that was cut and quarried in China. Both materials were shipped to San Francisco by sea. The cathedral served the Archdiocese of San Francisco from 1854 to 1891.

Alemany's successor, Archbishop Riordan, oversaw the construction of a new St. Mary's Cathedral on Van Ness Avenue that was completed in 1893. The following year, "Old St. Mary's," as it quickly came to be known, was given over to the Missionary Society of St. Paul the Apostle (also known as the Paulists). They continued to hold regular services for the parrish and established a Chinese mission there, which was originally housed in the cathedral's basement, but was moved to a house on Clay Street prior to the 1906 earthquake.

The devastating fire that followed the 1906 quake gutted the cathedral, melting its bell and destroying its roof, stained glass windows, marble detailing, and ceiling. The structure was rebuilt and rededicated in 1909, then remained relatively unchanged until a sacristy, transept, and three chapels were added in 1929. Designated a California Registered Historical Landmark in 1966, the cathedral is currently undergoing costly renovations to preserve it for future generations, including seismic retrofitting and structural reinforcement of the bell tower.

# Grace Cathedral

High atop Nob Hill, the third-largest Episcopal cathedral in the United States shares its lofty domain with other registered historical landmarks, including the Flood Mansion, the Fairmont Hotel, and the Mark Hopkins Hotel. Grace Cathedral sits upon land donated by the son of railroad baron Charles Crocker for the establishment of a new diocesan cathedral. Crocker's estate had previously occupied the land, but was completely destroyed by the 1906 earthquake and fire. English architect George Bodley, and later his partner, Cecil Hare, provided preliminary designs for the new cathedral. Local architect Lewis P. Hobart took over the project in 1910 and, after a study tour of European ecclesiastical architecture, returned with a new design incorporating French Gothic elements.

In 1910, the cornerstone of Grace Cathedral was officially laid, and the cathedral's first dean, Rev. J. Wilmer Gresham, was appointed to what would become almost 30 years of service. The Founders' Crypt opened in 1914 and served as a temporary cathedral until 1933. Lewis Hobart's second revision of the cathedral design, which utilized steel and reinforced concrete, was accepted in 1925, and construction resumed in 1927 with the Chapel of Grace. Great Depression economics halted construction during the early '30s, but building resumed in 1936 with construction of the Singing (north) Tower, completed in 1941. Construction halted again during World War II and did not resume until 1961.

Grace Cathedral opened to the public on November 20, 1964, with a huge televised consecration ceremony led by Bishop Pike and attended by many notable national and civic leaders. The church features an enormous faceted-glass rose window entitled *Canticle of the Sun*, designed by Gabriel Loire, as well as a casting of Renaissance sculptor Lorenzo Ghiberti's famed *Doors of Paradise*. Many visitors come to Grace Cathedral just to walk the meditative outdoor labyrinth, a replica of the thirteenth-century labyrinth laid in the floor of Chartres Cathedral in France. Regular music concerts held inside the cathedral offer another good excuse to make a trip to view this stunning structure.

*Grace Labyrinth.*

*Swedenborgian Church's garden, in which are planted trees from all over the world.*

## Swedenborgian Church

Originally named the Church of the New Jerusalem, the Swedenborgian Church (as it became known after the 1960s) is a testament to the vision and design aesthetics of Joseph Worcester, the church's first pastor.

Worcester was an East Coast Swedenborgian pastor and theologian who came to northern California in 1863 for health reasons. He had a strong interest in architecture and was deeply inspired by the writings of John Ruskin, an early promoter of the Arts and Crafts movement. Worcester's friendship with naturalist John Muir further helped to nurture in him a philosophy that strove to create harmony between nature and architectural design. In 1876, Worcester designed his own house in Piedmont, California, recognized today as the first Arts and Crafts

structure in the state. He also contributed to the designs of several other homes in San Francisco's Russian Hill neighborhood.

The visionary minister was well connected in the San Francisco architectural scene. Many noted architects of the time, including John G. Howard, Ernest Coxhead, A. Page Brown, and Willis Polk, incorporated the aesthetics of Worcester's Arts and Crafts movement into their own designs. Architect A. Page Brown was commissioned to design the Swedenborgian Church, with additional design contributions by Albert Cicero Schweinfurth, Bernard Maybeck, Bruce Porter, and William Keith, who painted the church's four interior murals. The church was recently listed on the National Register of Historic Places.

*Holy Virgin Cathedral*

San Francisco's Richmond District is home to a large Russian-speaking community that began to populate the neighborhood after World War I. Holy Virgin Cathedral (officially called the Cathedral of the Mother of God "Joy of All Who Sorrow") serves the district's Russian Orthodox community and includes an Orthodox academy and Russian high school.

The cathedral was founded in the early 1960s by St. John (Maximovich), Archbishop of Shanghai and San Francisco, a revered saint in the Eastern Orthodox Church who is also known as "the Wonderworker of Shanghai and San Francisco." Architect Oleg N. Ivanitsky is credited with design of the opulent church, completed in 1965. Crowned by five onion domes covered in 24-karat gold leaf, the church stands out noticeably from the rather bland architecture of the surrounding residential neighborhood and is especially dazzling when sunlight hits the towering golden domes. World-renowned iconographer Archimandrite Kiprian Pishew of Jordanville, New York, painted the church's interior frescos. Gold leaf tiles, icons, and mosaics can also be found throughout the cathedral, and a glass box contains the uncorrupted remains of St. John the Wonderworker.

There are no seats or pews in the large church, as Russian Orthodox services require attendants to stand for the duration of the mass (which normally lasts from 2 to 3 hours). The cathedral is open to the public only during mass times, and lay visitors are requested to wear proper attire and refrain from talking, taking photographs, or participating in the mass.

# First Unitarian Universalist Church of San Francisco

*Sarcophagus of Thomas Starr King.*

Unitarian services were first held in San Francisco beginning in 1850. Both of the fast-growing community's first two churches have been demolished, but the third is a registered landmark, constructed from 1887 to 1889 at the corner of Franklin and Geary. Architect George W. Percy designed the Gothic Revival-Romanesque sandstone church with radiant stained-glass rose windows. The building originally featured a steeple and bell tower, but these were destroyed by the 1906 earthquake and subsequently replaced with the square turret seen today. The interior features a hand-carved wood beam ceiling with wrought-iron and gilt chandeliers. In 1968, administration offices, meeting rooms, an education wing, and a chapel were added, all designed by architect Charles Warren Callister.

The sarcophagus of Thomas Starr King in First Unitarian's churchyard is a California Registered Historical Landmark, and a small plaque there commemorates his role in state history during the Civil War. King was a popular minister to the congregation from 1860 until his untimely death four years later. During the Civil War years, he traveled throughout California lecturing against slavery and the Confederacy, and is revered for his medical fundraising efforts for injured Union troops through the American Sanitary Commission, a precursor of the Red Cross.

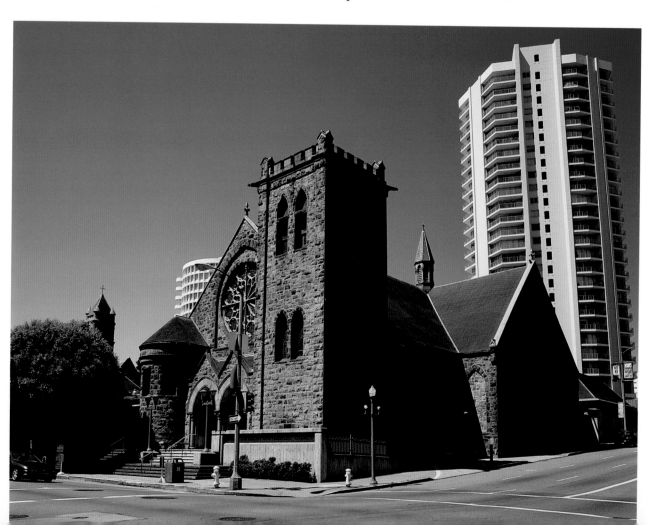

## Temple Emanu-El

Rosh Hashanah was first celebrated in San Francisco—indeed, on the West Coast—by a small group of roughly thirty Jews in a wood-framed tent on the 700 block of Montgomery Street in 1849. The city's first two congregations were chartered the following year: Temple Emanu-El ("God Is with Us") had congregants from Germany and central Europe, and Sherith Israel ("Remnant of Israel") served Jews from Prussian Poland and Eastern Europe.

Temple Emanu-El's current home at Lake Street and Arguello Boulevard in the Richmond District is the third site occupied by the Reform congregation. The imposing edifice there was designed by Arthur Brown Jr., a local architect. Brown had designed San Francisco City Hall in 1915, and he went on to design many other landmark buildings in San Francisco after the

synagogue, most notably Coit Tower on Telegraph Hill and the War Memorial Opera House and Veteran Building in Civic Center.

In 1927, the year after Emanu-El was completed, the American Institute of Architects declared it the finest piece of architecture in Northern California. The building incorporates architectural elements found in Istanbul's Hagia Sophia and other Byzantine domed structures. Underneath its 150-foot dome, the synagogue's Main Sanctuary is a dazzling yet peaceful space. Colored light from the sanctuary's many stained glass windows creates a dramatic effect on the prominent ark located at the end of the space. The temple features an ear-popping 4,500-pipe organ, as well as an impressive collection of rare works of Judaica housed in the Jacob Voorsanger Library.

# Lotta's Fountain

Located on a pedestrian island at the intersection of Geary, Market, and Kearny Streets, this ornate public fountain was given to the people of San Francisco as a gift by popular vaudeville celebrity Lotta Crabtree in 1875. Charlotte Mignon "Lotta" Crabtree started her illustrious career singing and dancing in mining camp taverns throughout northern California during the Gold Rush. By 1859, she had established herself as "Miss Lotta, the San Francisco favorite." When she formally retired in 1892, she was the highest-paid touring vaudeville performer in the country.

Lotta's beacon-like fountain was cast in Philadelphia and shipped to San Francisco via the Cape Horn route. It was spared the ravages of the 1906 earthquake and fire, and, in the aftermath of the disaster, quickly established itself as a meeting place and makeshift information center for survivors. Since then, it has been a symbol of the city's strength and resilience, much like other surviving landmarks.

In 1915, the fountain was heightened by eight feet; one year later, a series of bas-relief ornaments created by the brilliant local sculptor Arthur Putnam was added. The recently restored fountain plays annual host to small gatherings of dedicated San Franciscans who arrive at 5:13 a.m. every April 18 to remember and honor those who perished in the 1906 disaster.

## Mechanics Monument

Long recognized as a symbol of teamwork, strength, and fortitude, this brawny figurative monument was commissioned by James M. Donahue to honor the memory of his father, the late industrialist Peter Donahue. Peter Donahue was an Irish-born blacksmith who arrived in San Francisco at the start of the Gold Rush in 1849. Despite his modest means, he went on to start the first foundry on the Pacific Coast, to manufacture the first printing press in the West, to build a city railway, and to found the San Francisco Gas Company, thus becoming by the 1870s one of the most wealthy industrialists in the nation.

The tribute to this remarkable man was unveiled on Market Street, at the intersection of Bush and Battery Streets, in 1901. It was created by another remarkable man, local deaf artist Douglas Tilden, who was labeled the "Michelangelo of the West" for his mastery of the human form and legacy of masterworks. The bronze statue itself features five muscled machine shop workers toiling over a gigantic "punch press" machine: a reference to Peter Donahue's early career as a printing press manufacturer. In the 1906 disaster, the monument's fountain and reflecting pool—since removed—were damaged, but the statue itself survived relatively unscathed. Surrounded by smoking ruins and carnage, it served as an inspirational symbol of strength and perseverance to the crippled city at the dawn of its long reconstruction period. Even today, when times are relatively good, the monument still evokes in many San Franciscans a sense of pride and enduring history.

## Pioneer Monument

The Pioneer Monument now stands at the Civic Center between the new main Public Library and the Asian Art Museum, but it was once located a block away on Marshall Square at the intersection of Hyde and Grove. The 1,000-ton bronze and granite monument was commissioned through a bequest of $100,000 by real estate magnate and philanthropist James Lick, who died in 1876. Lick envisioned his gift to the city as a series of statues depicting epochs in California's history.

Sculptor F. H. Happersberger created the civic monument, which consists of a central pedestal of granite topped with a bronze sculptural representation of the California state seal: Minerva, the Roman goddess of wisdom, stands with a shield in her hand and a grizzly bear at her feet. This centerpiece is surrounded by four smaller granite pedestals, each topped with bronze figurative statuary. In one corner stands the Roman goddess of agriculture; in the opposite corner, the Roman goddess of Commerce. The remaining two corners are occupied by more modern, Western representations: the statue entitled *49* features three miners panning for gold; across from it, *Early Days* depicts a Mexican vaquero valiantly watching the frontier as a Spanish mission padre beside him shakes an authoritative index finger at a submissive Native American who cowers at his feet.

Local Native American rights groups have formally complained about this last bronze tableau, and it has been a target for vandalism and graffiti over the years. The monument and surrounding bronze fence have recently been restored, but the vaquero is still missing the lariat he once held—stolen years ago.

# Dewey Monument

Union Square's 95-foot-tall centerpiece was designed by San Francisco-born sculptor Robert Aitken and architect Newton Tharp. Completed in 1903, the navy monument commemorates Admiral George Dewey's 1898 victory over the Spanish fleet at Manila Bay in the Philippines during the Spanish-American War. It also honors the late president William McKinley, who broke ground for the memorial in San Francisco in 1901, just three months prior to his assassination on September 4 of that same year.

After the death of President William McKinley, the *San Francisco Chronicle* sponsored a fundraiser for the Union Square monument and successfully garnered $20,000 for its construction. A contest was then held to select a sculpture worthy of the navy victory and the late president. Several submissions were received, but all were busts or full-figure representations of the late president—except for one.

Sculptor Robert Aitken studied at the Mark Hopkins Institute of Art under Arthur Matthews and Douglas Tilden, and later became an instructor there himself. The design Aitken submitted for the memorial was a bronze figure of a woman in full stride, holding a laurel wreath (symbolizing peace at the end of the war) in one hand and a trident (symbolizing the sea) in the other. This unique design won the contest, and the sculptor began its execution immediately. To pose for the statue, he chose the local beauty Alma de Bretteville, a student and artists' model at the Mark Hopkins Institute of Art. Alma would later marry sugar baron Adolph Spreckels and become one of the wealthiest women in America, as well as one of San Francisco's most generous benefactors.

On Thursday, May 14, 1903, a dedication ceremony was held in Union Square with President Theodore Roosevelt presiding. The Dewey Monument survived the great earthquake and fire of 1906, and was recently restored during the latest remodeling of Union Square.

# Coit Tower

Located at the peak of Telegraph Hill and surrounded by Pioneer Park, this 210-foot, reinforced-concrete cylindrical tower is a renowned San Francisco landmark. The Art Deco movement reached its height during the Great Depression, and so played heavily in the design sensibility of the 1933 structure. The tower commemorates Lillie Hitchcock Coit, heiress to the fortune of local financier Howard Coit, and was constructed using funds bequeathed to the city by the generous benefactress. Lillie Coit had a life-long admiration for the city's firefighters, and many local tales recall her brave childhood antics trying to help her beloved Knickerbocker Engine Co. No. 5, which later made her an honorary member.

The tower is considered by many to resemble an Art Deco fire-hose nozzle, but architects Arthur Brown Jr. and Henry Howard denied any such inspiration. Visitors are permitted inside the memorial, and an interior elevator provides access to an observation deck at the tower's apex that offers spectacular views of the city and the San Francisco Bay.

In 1934, the Public Works of Art Project employed 26 local artists and 19 assistants to paint murals throughout the interior walls of the tower. Covering 3,691 square feet of wall space, these *fresco buono* murals depict scenes of California agricultural production, food production, industry, and San Francisco city life. The vast majority of the frescos have been restored, except for a few located in the stairway exit to the observation deck. These murals, some of which depict Socialist labor and political themes, suffered damage from vandalism over the years and, sadly, had to be covered over to hide it. All of the frescos throughout the tower share a similar style that is associated with Mexican murals of the era, and a high level of craftsmanship is evident throughout the entire collection.

*A statue of Christopher Columbus welcomes visitors to one of San Francisco's most-recognized landmarks.*

# San Francisco Lone Sailor Memorial

Facing the northern entrance of the Golden Gate Bridge, the Lone Sailor Memorial is dedicated to the thousands of men and women of the Navy, Marine Corps, Coast Guard, and Merchant Marines who have crossed through the Golden Gate in defense of their country. San Francisco was a huge navy town during the early and mid-twentieth century. During World War II, the entire Pacific fleet used the Golden Gate as its point of embarkation. Bay Area installations included the Kaiser shipyard in Richmond, the Alameda Naval Air Station, the Hunter's Point Naval Shipyard, Mare Island Naval Shipyard in Vallejo, and the Oakland Army Base.

The original Lone Sailor was created by artist Stanley Bleifield for the U.S. Navy Memorial in Washington, D.C., where it was unveiled to the public in 1987. Through the efforts of a dozen local World War II veterans, $2.2 million in private funds were raised to construct a memorial plaza and to purchase a bronze casting of the Washington statue for San Francisco. The 7-foot-tall bronze seaman stands stoically in the center of a circular granite foundation that features an elegantly designed compass rose pattern. Along the perimeter of the platform, bronze relief plaques depict insignias of the four sea services. The new Pacific Coast memorial was dedicated in 2002 at Vista Point Outlook, near Fort Baker in Sausalito, and is part of the Golden Gate National Recreation Area.

## Holocaust Memorial

In Lincoln Park, not far from the Palace of the Legion of Honor, the public sculpture entitled *The Holocaust* memorializes those who lost their lives to the Nazi death machine of the 1930s and '40s. The life-size human figures in the concentration camp scene are cast in bronze and painted white. The haunting tableau consists of eleven nude bodies lying on the ground—obviously representing murdered victims in a death camp. A twelfth, clothed person stands a few feet away from the group of bodies, his back turned to them, looking out at the San Francisco Bay through a barbed-wire fence that is suspended between two wooden poles on either side of him.

The statue was created by New York-based sculptor George Segal and given to the city of San Francisco in 1984. George Segal was a celebrated sculptor who used an unusual technique that involved wrapping live models in plaster and gauze for the creation of molds. A plaster version of *The Holocaust* is housed in the Jewish Museum of New York. Segal died in 2000, but he lives on in his well-known works *Depression Breadline*, at the Franklin Delano Roosevelt Memorial in Washington, D.C., and *Gay Liberation*, at the Stanford University campus

## National AIDS Memorial Grove

With the passing of the National AIDS Memorial Grove Act of 1996, a section of Golden Gate Park formerly known as the De Laveaga Dell became the nation's first official AIDS memorial. The site was started in 1988 by a small group of San Francisco residents who envisioned a safe and sacred place in a natural setting where individuals personally touched by AIDS could mourn, meditate, and heal. The sanctuary is a living tribute to all who have been affected directly or indirectly by the global tragedy, and is often used for memorial services and vigils. A large stone disc called the Circle of Friends bears the engraved names of the grove's

donors, those who have died, and those who loved them. Updated regularly, the list continues to expand outward in a spiral configuration—a sobering reminder of the disease's dizzying, ever-widening ring of destruction.

San Francisco was particularly hard hit by AIDS during the genesis of the pandemic in the 1980s. In 1987, Cleve Jones and a group of volunteers started the AIDS Memorial Quilt at a small storefront in San Francisco. Maintained by the NAMES Project Foundation, the quilt now incorporates over 48,000 individual quilted panels, and, like the ring of names, continues to grow.

# Martin Luther King Jr. Memorial

Commemorating the life and legacy of the revered Civil Rights leader, this modern tribute in Yerba Buena Gardens is not just something to gaze at. It is designed in such a way that visitors feel as though they are actively participating in an emotional and transformational journey. The memorial is like a simple house made of giant blocks of Sierra granite, but with a 50-foot-tall waterfall as one of the structure's walls. Visitors enter the "house" at either side of the waterfall, following a walkway that takes them into a dark, narrow chamber directly behind the cascading waters. The chamber is lined with backlit photos chronicling the Civil Rights Movement and glass panels inscribed with Dr. King's inspiring words. Visitors usually get a little wet here, as a mist is created by the thundering wall of water on the open side of the chamber. The acoustics of the inner passageway accentuate the din of the roaring waterfall, adding to the experience. Both entrances display large glass plates inscribed with the following quotations from Dr. King:

*No, No, we are not satisfied, and we will not be satisfied until "justice rolls down like water, and righteousness like a mighty stream."*
*Washington, D.C., 1963*

*I believe that one day will come when all God's children from bass black to treble white will be significant on the constitution's keyboard.*
*San Francisco, CA, 1956*

# Columbarium

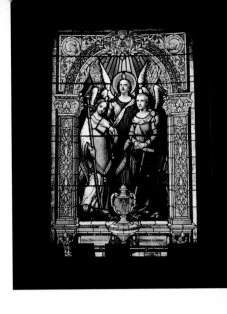

First constructed by the ancient Romans, *columbaria* are memorial structures used to house cinerary urns. The San Francisco Columbarium was designed by the British architect Bernard J. S. Cahill and built in 1898. The odd structure was commissioned by the Independent Order of Odd Fellows and was once part of the Odd Fellows Cemetery, which occupied over 150 acres of land in what is now the Richmond District. The cemetery once housed a crematory as well, but it was torn down in 1910 after a local law was passed prohibiting cremations in San Francisco.

Later, the City Beautiful Movement inspired legislation for the removal of all but two cemeteries located within the city limits. In 1930, the Odd Fellows Cemetery was removed and the remains of the thousands of deceased were relocated to newly constructed cemeteries outside the city limits, mostly in nearby Colma, California. The Columbarium was sold to Bay Cities Cemetery Association the same year, and five years later was declared a memorial under the Homestead Act. The site remained vacant for the next 45 years and was in dire need of repairs when the Neptune Society purchased the building in 1980.

The four-story, copper-domed Neoclassical building features a stained glass ceiling and several stained glass windows. Rows of niches contain urns housing the cremated remains of many distinguished—and not-so-distinguished—city residents. Mementos and photographs are sometimes placed in the niches as well, offering a glimpse into the lives and times of the deceased. Completely restored and renovated, the site was declared an official San Francisco landmark in 1995 and is open to the public today.

# Oases of Education and Entertainment: Museums, Performing Arts Centers, Cinemas, and Sports Parks

*Previous page: Lincoln Park golf course.*

*Opposite:* The Making of a Fresco Showing the Building of a City, *painted by Diego Rivera and students of the California School of Fine Arts in 1931.*

# San Francisco Art Institute

Founded in 1873, this renowned art school was established by the San Francisco Art Association, which was created two years earlier. The institute began as the California School of Design, but the name was changed to the California School of Fine Arts in 1916, then again to the San Francisco Art Institute in 1961. The school occupied four different buildings in the Nob Hill area before moving to its present location at 800 Chestnut Street in 1926.

The established local architectural firm of Blackwell and Brown designed the new school to resemble a medieval monastery, complete with bell tower and cloistered courtyard. The buildings in the complex all feature Italian and Spanish Colonial Revival architectural elements, such as ornate arches and

red tiled roofs. Skylights were added to some of the buildings to allow light into the artists' studios below.

Later additions to the building complex, designed by architect Paffard Keating Clay, were constructed in 1969. These include additional studio space, a theater and lecture hall, and an outdoor amphitheater. The school's gallery proudly displays a 1931 fresco entitled *The Making of a Fresco Showing the Building of a City*, painted by the celebrated Mexican muralist Diego Rivera and CSFA students.

The institute continues to furnish the world with a legacy of gifted artists and designers, as is evident from its distinguished list of alumni, which includes sculptor Gutzon Borglum (who carved Mt. Rushmore), photographer Annie Leibowitz, performance artist Karen Finley, and artist Jerome Caja.

# Exploratorium

Conceived and founded by noted physicist and educator Dr. Frank Oppenheimer, this renowned science museum has amazed and educated visitors since its opening in 1969. It has served as a working model for countless emerging and established science museums around the world. The museum is located in a large exhibition hall inside the Palace of Fine Arts, where it houses more than 600 interactive exhibits and welcomes over 50,000 visitors a year.

Human perception, science, art, and technology have been core areas of focus for the museum since its inception. Hands-on exhibits make learning about natural phenomena accessible and fun for young and old alike, and explore a wide range of subject areas, including touch, vision, sound, language, light, hearing, heat, electricity, weather, memory, and motion. The museum has three major departments: the Center for Public Exhibition makes sure that exhibits are relevant to modern science education and fit into a larger science curriculum; the Center for Teaching and Learning offers formal training programs for science and mathematics teachers, as well as children's educational outreach programs; the Center for Media and Communications uses interactive and traditional media to reach audiences outside the physical walls of the museum.

## San Francisco Museum of Modern Art

### (SFMOMA)

Established in 1935 as the San Francisco Museum of Art, this museum was the first on the West Coast to focus specifically on the acquisition and exhibition of modern twentieth-century art. In 1975, the word "modern" was officially added to the title to better describe the museum's emphasis. The museum was originally located in the War Memorial Veterans Building on Van Ness Avenue, but in 1995 moved into its new facility designed by Swiss architect Mario Botta in the South of Market District.

The museum houses thousands of twentieth-century masterpieces and boasts a permanent collection of more than 22,000 objects. There are departments for painting and sculpture, photography, architecture and design, and media arts. SFMOMA is renowned for its collection of distinguished paintings by artists associated with the American Abstract Expressionist School. It also contains a sizable collection of American Post-Minimalist, German Expressionist, and Fauvist works, along with an impressive collection of works by artists of the San Francisco Bay Area, southern California, and Mexico. Photographic holdings include major collections of works by renowned master photographers Alfred Stieglitz, Edward Weston, and Ansel Adams, as well as representative works by noted 1920s German Avant-Garde and 1930s European Surrealist photographers.

*SFMOMA's lobby.*

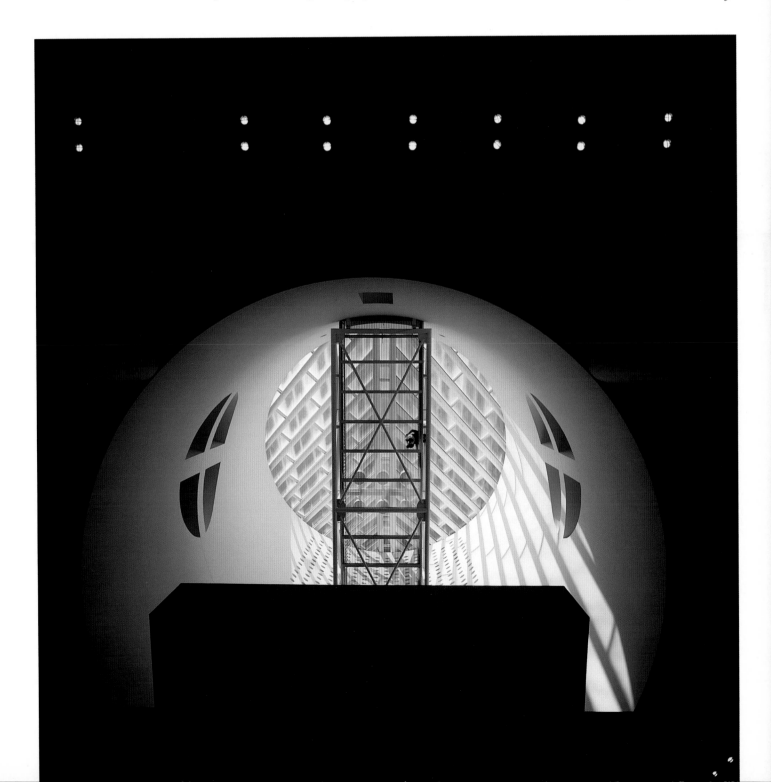

# Asian Art Museum of San Francisco

Focused specifically on the art of India, the Persian world, West Asia, Southeast Asia, the Himalayas, the Tibetan Buddhist world, China, Korea, and Japan, the Asian Art Museum of San Francisco is the largest museum of its kind in the United States and holds one of the most comprehensive collections of Asian art in the world. The museum opened in 1966 at its former location next to the M. H. de Young Memorial Museum in Golden Gate Park. It was originally called the Center for Asian Art and Culture, but was renamed in 1973.

The institution soon outgrew its park locale. In 1994, a local bond measure passed that provided funds for the city's old Main Library to be remodeled into a new home for the museum. Italian architect Gae Aulenti designed the architectural conversion of the 1917 Beaux Arts structure, and the new museum opened on March 20, 2003.

Over half of the 15,000 objects in the museum's collection were donated by Chicago industrialist Avery Brundage. In the early 1960s, Brundage made an initial donation to the city of San Francisco—a mere portion of his vast Asian art collection—that spawned the foundation of the museum. He continued to collect and make periodic donations until his death in 1975, at which time the remainder of his collection was bequeathed to the museum. Of particular note at the museum is a gilt bronze Buddha that dates to A.D. 338: the oldest known dated Chinese Buddha in the world.

## California Academy of Sciences

The California Academy of Sciences, begun in 1853 as the first scientific institution in the American West, is known today as one of the ten largest natural history museums in the world. The academy outgrew a number of locations during its early years as its collections of plants, animals, insects, minerals, and anthropological artifacts expanded—as did public desire to see the specimens on display.

The 1906 earthquake and fire destroyed the academy's popular six-story building at Market and Fourth Streets along with nearly all of its holdings. Over the next ten years, the organization successfully rebuilt its collection, and a new home was built for it in Golden Gate Park next to the Music Concourse in 1916. Later growth at the museum spurred additions to that site, including Steinhart Aquarium in 1923, Simson

African Hall in 1934, Morrison Planetarium in 1952, Cowell Hall in 1969, Wattis Hall in 1976, the Fish Roundabout in 1977, and the Life Through Time exhibit in 1990.

After the 1989 Loma Prieta earthquake caused structural damage to the building complex, plans were made for new museum buildings to be built at the same Golden Gate Park location. Pritzker Prize-winning architect Renzo Piano, in collaboration with the San Francisco-based firm of Gordon H. Chong and Partners, was chosen to design the new museum. The old museum closed in 2003, but a temporary facility opened to the public the following year at Fourth and Howard Streets in the South of Market District. Construction of the new museum is expected to be complete in 2008.

# California Palace of the Legion of Honor

Perched on a headland in Lincoln Park known as Land's End, this stately museum has astounding views of the Golden Gate. The museum was a philanthropic gift to the city of San Francisco by Adolph and Alma Spreckels, who commissioned architect George Applegarth to design the Beaux Arts building as a three-quarter-scale adaptation of the eighteenth-century Palais de la Legion d'Honneur in Paris. When it opened to the public on Armistice Day 1924, the museum was formally dedicated to the 3,600 Californians who died on the battlefields of France during World War I.

The museum features a large collection of ancient art, European decorative arts and paintings, and over seventy Rodin sculptures donated by Alma Spreckels, including the artist's famed *Thinker*, which greets visitors in the Court of Honor. The museum also houses one of the largest collections of rare prints and drawings in the United States. The palace is a member of the umbrella organization called the Fine Arts Museums of San Francisco.

## Musée Mecanique

Recently relocated from its former home under the historic Cliff House, the Musée Mecanique is now housed in an expanded warehouse facility on Pier 45 at Fisherman's Wharf. The museum boasts one of the largest collections of vintage arcade machines and mechanically operated musical instruments in the world. This site is a popular one among tourists at Fisherman's Wharf, and is especially loved by children. For longtime city residents, it has a special charm: they recognize many of the mechanical marvels from the now-demolished Playland-at-the-Beach, an amusement park on Ocean Beach that was in operation from the early 1920s until 1971.

The museum's collection was amassed by historian, philanthropist, and collector Ed Zelinsky, who died in 2004. It is currently maintained by his son, Dan. Zelinsky's collection of penny arcades and mechanical wonders includes many acquired from amusement king George Whitney's famed collection. From the 1930s to the 1950s, Whitney owned and operated three major attractions at Ocean Beach: the Cliff House restaurant, Playland-at-the-Beach, and the Sutro Baths and Museum. Today, only the Cliff House and the ruins of the once-magnificent Sutro Baths remain.

One of the museum's most popular attrac-tions is the locally famed "Laughing Sal," a six-foot-tall coin-operated mannequin originally from Playland's Fun House that has become the unofficial mascot of San Francisco. For 25 cents, the gap-toothed gal will convulse with hysterical laughter for a couple of minutes. Other fun pieces in the collection include antique player pianos and music machines of all types, animated dioramas, Mutoscopes (early moving-picture machines), 3D viewing machines, and mechanical fortune-tellers.

The same warehouse is also home to an exhibition of artifacts and photos sponsored by the San Francisco Museum and Historical Society. Entitled "Amusing America," the collection chronicles the history of American amusement and theme parks, world's fairs, arcades, swimming baths, and dance pavilions from the Gilded Age to the middle of the twentieth century.

*The "Old Barn Dance," with musical accompaniment by "the Mountain Boys."*

# San Francisco Maritime Museum

Since 1941, the unusual building in the heart of Aquatic Park across from Ghirardelli Square has housed a comprehensive collection of artifacts, documents, and photographs relating to the rich history of seafaring on the West Coast of America. The building was financed by the Works Progress Administration and designed by architects William Mooser Sr. & Jr. as a recreation center in 1939. Made of concrete, glass, and stainless steel, the Art Moderne architectural treasure resembles an ocean liner with chrome detailing and terrazzo floors. Tile murals by artist Hilaire Hiler depicting fantastic scenes of Atlantis were commissioned for the building's interior.

The museum's impressive collection includes model ships, painted mastheads, mast sections, and other maritime artifacts, along with educational videos, interactive displays, photo murals, and regularly updated exhibits that chronicle the maritime history of San Francisco and the West Coast. The Maritime Museum is one of several attractions in the San Francisco Maritime National Historic Park, and its open-air veranda offers wonderful views of some of the others, particularly Alcatraz Island and the historic vessels at Hyde Street Pier. Operated by the National Park Service, the museum is free and open daily year-round, and is also available for event rentals.

*Main-floor lobby of the Maritime Museum.*

*Above: These giant spindles power four underground cable loops, which pull all the city's cable cars.*

## Cable Car Museum

Established in 1974, the Cable Car Museum is located in a refurbished historic cable car barn and powerhouse at Washington and Mason Streets. The museum's observation deck allows visitors to see the large engines and cable winding wheels in action, while a lower-level viewing area lets them watch the enormous sheaves and cable lines entering the building. The museum's exhibits include cable car memorabilia, models, photographs, and ticket stub collections, as well as authentic cables, brakes, grips, and pieces of track. Three antique cable cars are on display, all dating to the 1870s. Among them

are both dummies and trailers: a dummy holds the train's grip mechanism, brakes, and a few passengers; trailers are the cars that are towed behind the dummy and which carry the majority of passengers.

One of those antique cable cars is the historic No. 8 grip car from Andrew Hallidie's Clay Street Hill Railroad, where the world's first public fleet of cable cars got its start in 1873. By the turn of the twentieth century, eight companies had established cable rail service lines throughout the city, and a network of over 53 miles of track was in operation. The cable rail system was severely damaged by the 1906 earthquake, and was soon thereafter rendered obsolete by the lower-cost electric streetcar. Luckily, San Franciscans were able to save some of their charming cable cars from extinction: After a major system-wide rehabilitation in the early 1980s, the California Line, the Powell-Mason Line, and the Powell-Hyde Line are today well loved by the thousands of tourists and locals who ride them every day.

*Sutter Street Dummy No. 46 and Trailer No. 54.*

*The Geary Theater and, on its right, the Curran Theater.*

## Geary and Curran Theaters

In the center of the city's theater district, just one block from Union Square, the Curran and the Geary have been entertaining San Francisco theatergoers for nearly a century. The first of the two to be constructed was the Geary Theater in 1910. American Conservatory Theater (ACT) has owned Geary since 1975, but it has been using the space as its home base since 1967. One year after ACT purchased the theater, it was officially listed on the National Register of Historic Places. Designed by the prominent architectural firm of Bliss & Faville, the gorgeous building features a yellow brick and glazed terracotta façade that incorporates Neoclassical and Baroque design elements.

The Curran Theater next door opened in 1922 as one playhouse in a chain of theaters run by Sam and Lee Shubert, the "dynamic duo" of Broadway at the time. Architect Alfred Henry Jacobs designed the $800,000 structure, whose exterior architectural detailing is every bit as opulent as the Geary's. The interior of the Curran features murals painted by artist Arthur Matthews and several elegant crystal chandeliers. San Francisco Civic Light Opera (SFCLO), an in-house theater company at the Curran, gets the credit for alleviating the city's dependence on imported shows from New York in the 1940s. In the late '70s, the theater was sold to Broadway producer Carole Shorenstein Hayes and business partner Scott E. Nederlander, who introduced the popular "Best of Broadway" series to its stage. Their Shorenstein Hays-Nederlander Organization also currently owns the Orpheum and Golden Gate Theatres.

# Orpheum Theatre

This decadent theater opened in 1926 as one in a chain of vaudeville houses owned by theatrical entrepreneur and businessman Alexander Pantages. The Spanish-style venue was designed by architect B. Marcus Priteca, an architectural historian and illustrator who was renowned for designing hundreds of fantastical and ornamental "theme theaters." The building's façade appropriates design elements from a twelfth-century cathedral in Leon; the Alhambra Palace in Granada, Spain, served as inspiration for the theater lobby's vaulted ceiling.

As vaudeville declined, so did Pantages's holdings, and he eventually sold the house to RKO (Radio-Keith-Orpheum), a film production company with theater chain operations across the country. The old vaudeville house was converted into a movie theater, and it served in that function for 35 years. Renamed the Orpheum Theatre,

it was one of many successful movie palaces that flourished along Market Street until the rise of television forced most to close. The Orpheum made several changes during the 1950s to try to stay alive, but it too ultimately closed.

The theater's return as a live performance venue occurred when American Conservatory Theater's production of the musical *Hair* opened at the Orpheum in 1970. After a four-year stint as home to the San Francisco Civic Light Opera (SFCLO), the theater was sold to the Shorenstein Hays-Nederlander Organization, whose "Best of Broadway" series at the Orpheum and other theaters has been thrilling locals for over two decades.

# Beach Blanket Babylon

Like fog, cable cars, and sourdough bread, *Beach Blanket Babylon* is a San Francisco institution—and it also happens to hold the record for the longest-running musical revue in American theater history. Created by the late Steve Silver, the show originally opened at the Savoy Tivoli in 1974, but soon thereafter moved to its current location at Club Fugazi in the city's North Beach District.

The zany, fast-paced musical revue features hilarious spoofs of celebrities and newsmakers of the day, and so is updated regularly. Audiences find great amusement in the show's colorful costumes and trademark oversized theme-hats, which have been created by veteran hat maker Alan Greenspan since 1978. The outrageous headdress creations include a 200-pound rendition of the city skyline—complete with Transamerica Pyramid,

*Bust of show creator Steve Silver.*

bridges, twinkling lights, and fog—which longtime star Val Diamond must balance on her head for the finale song "San Francisco" (from the 1936 Jeanette McDonald movie of the same name).

Show creator Steve Silver was a generous contributor to AIDS charities and Jewish philanthropic organizations during his later years of success. Since his death in 1995, his wife, Jo Schuman Silver, has been involved in the show's perpetuation. *Beach Blanket Babylon* continues to play to a packed house in San Francisco, and a traveling version of the production currently tours the globe.

*Below: Entrance to Club Fugazi, the show's home.*

Castro Theatre

A treasured fixture in the hearts of San Franciscans, this extravagantly designed movie palace has remained in operation since its grand opening on June 22, 1922. The Nasser Brothers, who had success with many nickelodeons throughout the Eureka Valley District of San Francisco, spent $300,000 on the theater's construction. As local architect Timothy L. Pflueger's first theater design, the ornate beauty of the Castro would catapult his career and lead to other major theater commissions.

The theater features an elegant Mexican Colonial-style façade, with an outdoor foyer and freestanding box office that are attractively decorated with glazed tiles. The interior lobby is flanked by two grand staircases leading up to a large mezzanine area and balcony seating. The 1,400-seat main auditorium is crowned by a large, metallic Art Deco chandelier that was added in 1937. Sgrafitto murals with Classical motifs adorn the auditorium walls, and the hand-painted canopy ceiling features a series of Far Eastern figures incorporated into a detailed mandalic design. One of the theater's most distinguished offerings is its mighty Wurlitzer organ, a replacement for the old Morton console that was retired in 1982. The Wurlitzer was custom-built by pipe organ enthusiasts Ray Taylor and his sons in the late 1970s, and is currently maintained by the American Theater Organ Society.

The landmark has recently benefited from extensive restoration and preservation efforts, such that only the richly painted auditorium ceiling—darkened from decades of tobacco smoke and peeling in parts—is still noticeably in need of repair and cleaning. The Castro has remained in the Nasser family to the present day, but they lease the theater to other managers.

## Wells Fargo History Museum

This fascinating museum in the heart of the Financial District chronicles the history of the Gold Rush and the important role Wells Fargo & Co. played in San Francisco banking and cross-country transportation during and immediately following that era. Some exhibits include California gold dust and vintage Gold Rush Era letters. The museum's centerpiece is one of the actual Concord stagecoaches that were built for Wells Fargo & Co. by master carriage builders J. Stephens Abbot and Lewis Downing in the 1860s.

Henry Wells and William G. Fargo and Associates founded the Wells Fargo firm in New York City in March of 1852. Four months later, they opened in San Francisco and Sacramento, and soon thereafter offices popped up in mining camps and boomtowns across the American West. The company assayed and bought gold, sold paper bank drafts, and most importantly, provided express mail delivery of customers' gold, valuables, and letters from San Francisco and Western frontier towns to the East Coast.

From 1875 to 1883, Wells Fargo & Co. was targeted by Black Bart, an infamous stagecoach robber with 29 successful robberies to his credit. The dreaded criminal's wanted posters were pasted all over the country. When he was found residing at 37 Second Street in San Francisco—only four blocks from Wells Fargo's West Coast headquarters—people were surprised at just how not scary he really was: He was Charles E. Boles, a mild-mannered former druggist who not only was afraid of horses, but who had never fired a bullet from his gun—because he never loaded it. After four years in San Quentin Prison, Boles renounced his life of crime to the press and vanished, never to be seen again.

In 1918, Wells Fargo & Co. decided to end its mail carrier service in order to focus on its banking business. Today, the institution is one of the nation's major players in banking and finance, with branches throughout the country. Its museum business is also nation-wide, counting eight in addition to the intriguing branch in San Francisco, all of which are no doubt worth a visit.

# M.H. de Young Memorial Museum

San Francisco's oldest museum, the de Young Museum as it is simply called today, sits in a beautiful natural setting within Golden Gate Park. Founded in 1895, the museum is named after Michael de Young, publisher of the *San Francisco Chronicle*, and originally served as a memorial museum to the successful California Midwinter International Exposition of 1894 which de Young helped to realize. Michael de Young, as head of the fair's Executive Committee, arranged for the Fine Arts building to be saved from demolition and gave the Egyptian Revival style structure to the Golden Gate Park commissioners, along with surplus profits from the fair, for the purpose of establishing a permanent museum. Originally simply a repository for artifacts from the fair, de Young began acquiring new objects for the museum soon after it opened in March of 1895. Known for his eclectic taste, de Young's acquisitions included paintings, sculpture, arms, armor, fine porcelain, and various artifacts of Native American and South Pacific cultures. Two wings were added to the museum by de Young before his death in 1925. The original Egyptian building was declared unsafe and replaced with a modest replica in 1931.

After 100 years, the museum has developed a reputation for its impressive collections of ancient art, American art from the Colonial period to the modern age, textiles, and arts of Africa, Oceania, and the Americas.

The museum suffered major structural damage from the 1985 Loma Prieta earthquake and was closed in 2000. A new museum building was designed by architects Herzog & de Meuron (best known for their design of the Tate Gallery in London) and opened in 2005.

*The new de Young museum—primary designer Herzog & de Meuron, principal architects Fong & Chan.*

# San Francisco War Memorial and Performing Arts Center

One of the nation's largest performing arts centers, the San Francisco War Memorial and Performing Arts Center is a complex of monumental buildings that line Van Ness Avenue for two and a half city blocks. The three cultural venues have become fixtures of the Civic Center Historic District.

The War Memorial Opera House and Veterans Building were both constructed in 1932. Architects Arthur Brown Jr. and G. Albert Lansburgh designed the two massive French Renaissance structures to complement the City Hall building across the street. They are clearly a pair: both of their interiors exhibit the trappings of the Beaux Arts style, with grand chandeliers, gold leafing, marble, and heavy ornamentation; outside they are connected by a small courtyard. The elegant 3,146-seat opera house is home to the San Francisco Opera and the San Francisco Ballet. The Veterans Building houses the 916-seat Herbst Theater, site of the signing of the United Nations charter in 1945. Eight large murals painted by Frank Bragwyn for the 1915 Panama-Pacific International Exhibition are featured on the auditorium walls.

To the left of the Opera House across Grove Street stands the more modern Louise M. Davies Symphony Hall, built in 1980. Its design successfully incorporates many of the architectural elements found in the surrounding buildings. The hall has been home to the San Francisco Symphony since its opening.

# SBC Park

Located on the waterfront near China Basin and the Lefty O'Doul Bridge, this 41,000-seat stadium is the city's new home for the San Francisco Giants. After nearly three years of construction, the ballpark finally held its first game on March 31, 2000: an exhibition game between the Giants and the Milwaukee Brewers that turned out to be the home team's first win in its new home. So far, Giants fans' most memorable moment at SBC is when Barry Bonds hit his five-hundredth home run there on April 17, 2001, making him the seventeenth player in Major League baseball to reach the 500 mark.

The park was designed by the Kansas-based architectural firm HOK Sport as an open-air stadium, but is crafted to resist the strong winds from the San Francisco Bay—a feature that Candlestick Park couldn't provide. Two red-brick clock towers flank

the entrance to the ballpark on King Street, and a public promenade runs along the waterfront behind the stadium.

The structure is one of many redevelopments promoted by the city in the South Beach area, an industrial section of town that is rapidly becoming gentrified. Private financing built the new $255 million stadium, which is owned by the China Basin Ballpark Corp., a subsidiary of the Giants. SBC Park was originally called Pac Bell Park, but SBC Communications, Inc. acquired Pacific Bell soon after the park was built and changed its name.

*San Francisco left fielder, Barry Bonds, looks at the list of homerun leaders after hitting his 661st home run at SBC Park, thereby surpassing Willie Mays on the all-time career home runs list.*

## Candlestick Park

In 1958, the New York Giants moved to San Francisco and changed their name to the San Francisco Giants. For their first season out West, they played at Seals Stadium, but in 1960, the brand new Candlestick Park stadium welcomed them home. For forty years, they played at this windy park designed by architect John Bolles, until they moved into the newly constructed Pac Bell Park near China Basin in the South of Market District. Candlestick is still home to the San Francisco '49ers, who played their first football game there in 1971. Since its construction,

the stadium has been expanded several times; it is currently undergoing renovation to increase the seating capacity to 71,000.

Candlestick Park has always been owned by the City of San Francisco and managed by the Recreation and Park Department. Its name, on the other hand, has changed several times: From 1995 to 2002, the stadium was called 3Com Park, after the 3Com Corporation agreed to pay the city nearly $4 million for naming rights. Soon after that contract expired, Monster Cable Products, Inc. entered into a similar naming rights

deal with the city, and the stadium is now to be called Monster Park until 2008. In 2004, however, city voters passed a measure stating that the name "Candlestick Park" be reinstated permanently after 2008.

Over the years, Candlestick Park has earned itself quite a reputation. It is well known to fans of the Beatles, who played their last concert at the venue on August 29, 1966. During the 1989 World Series game between the Giants and the Oakland A's, Candlestick received much more media attention than even

a World Series would normally warrant: just as game three was commencing, the Loma Prieta earthquake struck, stunning not only those in the park, but also millions of live television viewers. Lesser known is the origin of the stadium's beloved name: nearby Candlestick Point, which got its name from the candlestick bird, an indigenous wading bird common in the San Francisco Bay area before the 1950s. A large flock of these birds inhabited Candlestick Cove until hunting drove the chicken-like fowl to near extinction.

The Multicultural Metropolis:
Unique Neighborhoods,
Streets, and Squares

*Previous page: Fisherman's Wharf.*

*Above: Chinatown Gate, a gift to the city of San Francisco from the Republic of Taiwan, erected in 1970.*

## Chinatown

As home to the nation's second-largest Chinese community, this colorful neighborhood has a rich history and cultural heritage—not to mention a charm and exotic appeal that are a major draw to tourists. The history of Chinese immigration to California begins in 1849, when news of the discovery of gold at Sutter's Mill shot out from the state to all four corners of the earth. Many Chinese who were fed up with the famine and political unrest in their native land decided to leave everything behind and seek their fortune in the "Golden Mountains" of northern California. These early immigrants were met with hostility and suspicion in the mines and soon made their way back to San Francisco to find work and housing.

There, Chinese immigrants were met with prejudice and discriminatory laws during the late nineteenth and early twentieth centuries, but their insulated and self-sufficient ethnic neighborhood was able to thrive nevertheless. Chinese benevolent societies formed in the 1850s, and at that time the district was granted some degree of autonomy. Opium, prostitution, and Chinese gang violence were common problems in Chinatown during the rough and rowdy Barbary Coast Era of the late nineteenth and early twentieth centuries. The neighborhood was completely destroyed during the 1906 earthquake and fire, and most of the structures seen today were created by American architects in an Orientalist style during the city's reconstruction period.

When the first Chinese immigrants arrived in San Francisco from the mines, they settled only along the perimeter of Portsmouth Square, the city's first public square and civic center. Eventually, however, their neighborhood grew to encompass the eight-block area it occupies today, defined by Broadway, California, Kearny, and Powell Streets. Grant and Stockton Streets are the district's main thoroughfares and are connected by several small alleyways. Both streets are lined with Chinese restaurants, souvenir shops, antique stores, clothing and textile stores, herbal medicine shops, and food markets.

# Fisherman's Wharf

Along with Alcatraz Island and Chinatown, Fisherman's Wharf is one of the city's most popular tourist attractions. The neighborhood stretches the length of Jefferson Street between Powell and Hyde Streets and includes the northernmost section of the Embarcadero. Bounded to the west by the Marina and to the south by North Beach, the seven-block strip abounds with sidewalk seafood vendors, restaurants, waterfront attractions, souvenir shops, and hotels. The vibrant atmosphere that distinguishes Fisherman's Wharf is kept alive by street performers and musicians, crab vendors calling for customers, the invigorating smell of the sea, and the dazzling lights and neon signs that illuminate the area at night. The condensed main strip is a magnet for large crowds of tourists; locals generally consider it too crowded and avoid it.

Fisherman's Wharf has been home to San Francisco's fishing fleet since the post-Gold Rush Era of the mid-nineteenth century. By the turn of the twentieth century, Italian immigrants, mostly skilled Genoese and Sicilian fishermen, were firmly established in the area. In those days, the docks were filled with feluccas—small sailboats commonly found throughout the Mediterranean—interspersed by a small number of Chinese junks. These first-generation sailboats were soon replaced by the gasoline-powered crafts known locally as Monterey Hull boats. With the approach of modernization, these boats were replaced by the diesel-powered commercial vessels in use today.

During the late nineteenth and early twentieth centuries, the relatively small, predominantly Italian fishing port began to expand and diversify. Restaurants soon emerged, and San Francisco's reputation for fresh, quality seafood of all types spread worldwide. The modern wharf is now teeming with seafood restaurants; some family-run operations have been in business for over half a century already. Beginning in the 1950s and '60s, many of the wharf's historic buildings were modernized and converted into retail spaces. The buildings at Ghirardelli Square—originally the Pioneer Woolen Mill, then the Ghirardelli

*Sea lions at Pier39's "K" dock.*

Chocolate Factory—were converted into the busy shopping and dining complex one sees today. Similarly, in 1966, the brick-walled Del Monte peach cannery at the foot of Columbus Street was recycled into a three-level shopping, dining, and theater complex now known simply as the Cannery. Pier 39, another shopping, dining, and entertainment complex which opened to the public in 1978, was built with recycled wood from Piers 3 and 34.

The wharf also offers three popular amusement museums: Musée Mecanique, Ripley's Believe It or Not! Museum, and the Wax Museum on Jefferson Street, which is one of the largest wax museums in the world. Two floating memorial museums at Pier 45 focus specifically on mar-

itime history: the historic ships S.S. *Jeremiah O'Brien*, a fully restored and operational World War II Liberty ship, and the *U.S.S. Pampanito*, a World War II Balao-class fleet submarine. The Fisherman's and Seaman's Memorial, a small chapel on Pier 45, pays tribute to the generations of hard-working San Franciscan seafarers who have battled the elements in search of the sea's bounty for over 150 years.

As if that weren't enough to entertain San Francisco's guests, large numbers of California sea lions unexpectedly began to make Pier 39's "K" dock their permanent residence in 1990. Nearly 1,000 of the charming sea mammals still call the dock home and daily amuse onlooking tourists with their wet-and-wild antics.

# North Beach

Situated between Chinatown and Fisherman's Wharf, the charming neighborhood of North Beach—also known as Little Italy—is a lively area filled with outdoor cafés, nightclubs, bookstores, and high-end boutiques, as well as plenty of Italian restaurants, delicatessens, and bakeries. The area was once part of the old Barbary Coast and became a haven for Italian immigrants beginning in the late 1880s. During the 1950s and '60s, the neighborhood's image took a sharp turn when it became associated with Beat-generation poets and writers such as Alan Ginsberg, Jack Kerouac, and William S. Burroughs.

North Beach is home to several notable sites. The Sentinel Building, a registered landmark, is located there, as is the Neo-Gothic Saints Peter and Paul Church, which holds an annual procession to Fisherman's Wharf for the "Blessing of the Fishing Fleet." Washington Square Park marks the heart of the neighborhood and offers a square block of lush lawn space and magnificent views of Telegraph Hill and Coit Tower. North Beach has its own historical museum on Stockton near Columbus Avenue, with vintage photographs and artifacts that chronicle the neighborhood's rich past.

*Saints Peter and Paul Church on Washington Square.*

# Jackson Square Historic District

Avirtual reliquary of San Francisco's earliest commercial buildings, the Jackson Square Historic District is cherished for its authentic Barbary Coast feel. In the 1850s, the area was actually the waterfront, but the water was later replaced with landfill. The new foundation, consisting primarily of sand and the remains of wooden ships abandoned by eager gold prospectors headed for the mines in northern California, was soon utilized for the construction of hundreds of commercial and office buildings. Most of the structures are only one story tall and commonly feature Italianate façades, sturdy brickwork, and cast iron embellishments. The Jackson Square area was officially designated a San Francisco Historic District in the 1950s. Today, the historic buildings that grace the tree-lined streets and alleys of this charming neighborhood are considered prime commercial real estate and are thriving as high-end antique shops, fine art galleries, and designer showrooms.

# Castro District

What is known today as the quintessential "gay mecca" of the world was once known humbly as Eureka Valley, a working-class neighborhood of Irish, German, and Scandinavian immigrant families. The neighborhood was begun in the late 1880s, and most of the homes here were built during the late nineteenth and early twentieth centuries. After World War II, San Francisco experienced a massive population exodus as families left the hectic city for suburbs.

As a result of the exodus, many of the Victorian homes in the Castro District became quite affordable during the 1960s and '70s, and a large number of gay homebuyers took advantage of the opportunity to restore the

classic homes to their original grandeur. The Gay Liberation Movement blossomed in the neighborhood, and a sense of community developed that culminated with the opening of Twin Peaks, the city's first gay bar to feature a glass façade, and the election of Harvey Milk, the city's first openly gay district supervisor. Milk's assassination in 1978 and the emergence of the AIDS pandemic around the same time spurred much activism in the Castro Disrict during the late '70s and throughout the '80s.

Castro Street between Twentieth and Seventeenth Streets is the neighborhood's main strip and features several gay bars, clothing stores, novelty shops, restaurants, and the historic landmark movie palace, the Castro Theatre. The neighborhood hosts a popular annual street fair and is packed to full capacity with partygoers on Halloween and on the eve of the annual GLBT (Gay, Lesbian, Bisexual, Transsexual) Pride Parade, known locally as "Pink Saturday."

*710 Ashbury Street, home of the Grateful Dead in the 1960s.*

## Haight-Ashbury District

One of San Francisco's most famed neighborhoods, the Haight-Ashbury District is best known for its role as the epicenter of hippie culture during the late 1960s. The district covers nearly 30 blocks that are bounded by Stanyan Street and Golden Gate Park to the west, the Golden Gate Park Panhandle to the north, Central Avenue and Buena Vista Park to the east, and Fredrick Street to the south. The neighborhood's streets were named in the late 1860s, many of them after prominent political and civic leaders of the day. Haight Street, the main commercial strip in the district, was named after

banker and California governor Henry Haight, who donated land in the area for a Protestant orphanage, in operation between 1854 and 1920. Ashbury Street is named after San Francisco Park Commissioner Monroe Ashbury. The district was named for the popular intersection of these two busy streets.

Haight-Ashbury is filled with Victorian- and Queen Anne-style residences that were constructed for middle-class families during the late nineteenth and early twentieth centuries. After the Great Depression of the 1930s, the neighborhood went into a period of noticeable decline. By the

*Mural of Jim Morrison and Janis Joplin in the Haight-Ashbury District.*

1960s, the general state of disrepair here had driven rents way down, thus creating fertile ground for low-income, counterculture youth—that is, hippies. After the Human Be-In festival in Golden Gate Park and the 1967 Summer of Love launched the flower-power, anti-Vietnam War counterculture into national headlines, the hippie movement gained in popularity among the nation's youth, and Haight-Ashbury became a magnet for like-minded peace-and-love movement devotees, psychadelic-drug enthusiasts, musicians, artists, and teen runaways from around the country, and even around the world.

In 1969, hard drugs entered the scene and pretty much ended the bohemian peace-and-love party. Increasing violence led to more economic decline in the neighbor-hood during the 1970s. Since the 1980s, however, Haight-Ashbury has undergone a substantial degree of gentrification, with real estate prices now quite high. Haight Street itself has become a popular destination for tourists who relish the street's assortment of vintage clothing and novelty shops, record stores, incense and smoke shops, restaurants, and dive bars.

## Alamo Square Historic District

This hilltop residential neighborhood surrounds Alamo Square Park in the Western Addition District. The area contains hundreds of historic homes dating from the 1870s to the 1920s, including several registered historic landmark properties, like the Westerfeld House and the Archbishop's Mansion, both located on Fulton Street.

Alamo Square Park was formally dedicated as a public space in 1858, but it was avoided by most

locals until the city ousted the notorious squatter and outlaw "Dutch Charlie" Duane from the premises ten years later. Grading, landscaping, and the construction of curved pathways, stairways, and a retaining wall were completed in 1892. The park served as a refuge for homeless locals after the 1906 earthquake and fire demolished most of the city. From the 1950s to the 1970s, the area was in a period of decline, with most of the homes in the neighborhood in need of restoration and

crime rampant in the park and surrounding streets. Regular police patrols helped restore the neighborhood to a relative degree of safety in the early '80s. In 1982, the 12-block area surrounding Alamo Square Park was declared a registered historic district, and soon thereafter the majority of the homes in the neighborhood were lovingly restored by their owners.

Today, the upscale neighborhood boasts some of the most beautiful and expensive real estate in the city. Best known—or, at least, most often seen—is the string of Victorian homes that lines Steiner Street on the east side of the park, looming above the modern metropolis in the background. The picturesque scene contrasting old and new San Francisco has been used countless times in photo postcards, hence the street's local nickname, "Postcard Row."

# Lombard Street

One of San Francisco's most cherished oddities is the one-block section of Lombard Street on Russian Hill. Since its creation in the early 1920s, the block has been promoted by locals and known worldwide as "the Crookedest Street in the World." The steep, forty-degree slope in the hill necessitated the incorporation of eight extremely sharp turns in the road, creating a curious zigzag effect. The road's strangeness is emphasized by the two pedestrian walkways that flank it—both of which are straight. The rest of Lombard Street continues in straight lines, west to the Presidio and east to the Embarcadero.

Although Lombard is always a big draw to motorists who want to be able to say that they have driven down "the Crookedest Street in the World," the road is actually not the most crooked in the world. It's not even the most crooked in San Francisco: there are steeper and much more crooked streets in the City of Hills. The fact that, out of all of them, Lombard Street remains a local icon and such a popular attraction for visitors is probably due more to its quaintness than its curviness. Lined with brick and accented with lush shrubs and flowers, the picturesque winding road has always been a favorite image for tourist postcards and, along with the Transamerica Pyramid Building, the Golden Gate Bridge, and Alcatraz, stands as one of the city's most recognizable landmarks. The hill offers spectacular scenic views of North Beach, Coit Tower, and the San Francisco Bay. To top it off, the surrounding Russian Hill District is primarily an upper-class neighborhood, consisting of expensive Victorian mansions, classy townhouses, and gorgeous condominiums.

# Union Square

Proclaimed a public square in 1850 by the city's first mayor, John White Geary, this 2.6-acre block bordered by Powell, Post, Stockton, and Geary Streets was the center of town during the pioneer days—and remains so to the present day. The name of the square originated in 1860, when it was a popular spot for pro-Union rallies just prior to the start of the Civil War.

During the heyday of the fabled Barbary Coast, a two-block crib-alley called Morton Street, located directly across from the square, was quite notorious. Prostitutes there would brazenly display what they had to offer through open windows, inviting the often inebriated passersby to touch one breast for ten cents, or both for a nickel more. For ten cents to a dollar more, the gents were allowed inside. After the 1906 earthquake and fire, the street was renamed Maiden Lane.

In 1903, President Theodore Roosevelt came to Union Square to dedicate a newly built, 97-foot monument commemorating Admiral Dewey's victory at Manila Bay in the Philippines. The monument still stands today in the center of the square, but the layout of Union Square has otherwise been modified many times in its 150-plus years of existence. Currently, it consists of a 245-foot-long granite plaza with steps, ledges, benches, and small patches of grass. There are entrances to the square at each of its four corners, and Canary Island palm trees line the perimeter. A plan for the addition of a water fountain is in the works. Every December, the square is host to an enormous glittering Christmas tree and to a large menorah.

Since 1945, most of the historic buildings surrounding Union Square have been either demolished or rebuilt beyond recognition. Two notable exceptions are the 1904 St. Francis Hotel and the 1908 Elkan Gunst Building, both on Powell Street. The Nieman Marcus store one sees today on the corner of Geary and Stockton Streets is something of an architectural compromise. The stunning City of Paris department store was demolished in 1970 to make room for the new Neiman Marcus store, but architect Philip Johnson ingeniously preserved and incorporated the original building's rococo plaster ornamentation and exquisite stained glass and gold-trimmed rotunda into the new building.

Aside from these few exceptions, modern buildings have taken over most of the square block, occupied by department store giants like Macy's Union Square (the largest department store west of New York City) and Saks Fifth Avenue. Of particular interest to enthusiasts of the Modern style is San Francisco's only Frank Lloyd Wright building, the Circle Gallery (formerly the Morris Store) on Maiden Lane. Its curved interior is considered a precursor to Wright's later design of the Guggenheim Museum in Manhattan.

Union Square continues to be a welcome respite for the tired feet of "shop-till-you-drop" consumers, as well as for tourists and locals who just like to observe the hustle and bustle of the busy shopping district. Also, the glass elevators installed in the St. Francis Hotel's modern tower offer breathtaking birds-eye views of the square and its surroundings that are not to be missed.

# Market Street

arket Street began as a distinct thoroughfare in the 1850s. It originally stretched from the Ferry Building on the eastern shoreline to just beyond the downtown area, but has grown to its current span across half of the city, from the Ferry Building to Twin Peaks. In the 1860s, Market Street replaced Montgomery Street as the preferred avenue for parades and

pageants—a tradition that continues to this day—and soon established itself as the main artery of the city. The historic portion of Market Street runs from the Ferry Building to Van Ness Avenue and passes through the busy Financial District, Downtown, and the Civic Center District. Many prominent landmarks, including the Palace Hotel, Lotta's Fountain, Samuel's

*Opposite and above: Vintage trolleys on the Market Street line.*

Clock, the Flatiron Building, the Phelan Building, the Hobart Building, the Flood Building, and the Orpheum Theatre, can be found along this eleven-block section of Market Street.

Market Street and the streets of the South of Market District run at an odd angle to the rest of the city's streets, which generally follow a north-south grid. Market's northeast-southwest direction can make directional orientation difficult for newcomers. Luckily for tourists, it's actually much more enjoyable to ride the public trans-portation in this area than to drive oneself. The F-line, the world's longest-publicly operated heritage streetcar line, operates daily along Market Street, up the Embarcadero, and over to Fisherman's Wharf. The line features 30 vintage restored streetcars, trolleys, and trams from around the globe. The Market and Powell Street intersection marks the center of the city's shopping district and is the point of embarkation for historic cable cars running north to Fisherman's Wharf.

What a Beautiful Day!
Parks and Recreation

*Previous page: Ocean Beach.*

*Opposite: The Dutch Windmill, located in Golden Gate Park's Queen Wilhelmina Tulip Garden.*

# Golden Gate Park

Golden Gate Park is San Francisco's largest urban public park, surpassing with its more than 1,000 acres even the size of New York City's Central Park. It's a little more awkwardly shaped than Central Park, though, with a skinny, one-block-wide, eight-block-long section that protrudes from the eastern border of the large, nine-block-wide, three-mile-long midsection. This strange distribution of land makes the whole area look very much like a big green frying skillet, hence the local nickname for the protrusion: "the Panhandle." The wider "pan" portion of Golden Gate Park stretches from Stanyan Street in the Haight-Ashbury District eastward to the Great Highway and Pacific Ocean.

William Hammond Hall became the park's first superintendent in 1871. He is credited with designing the park's roads and paths through what was, at that time, nothing more than acres of sand dunes. When his successor, John McLaren, took over the project in 1887, he pushed for the sandy park's development into a friendlier habitat for trees and plants. He and his successors succeeded well in this endeavor: the park is now full of sprawling gardens and meadows, crystalline bodies of water, forested areas, and all manner of wildlife. Areas of particular natural beauty at the park include the Queen Wilhelmina Tulip Garden, the Rose Garden, the Fragrance Garden, and the Shakespeare Garden. Stow Lake, the most popular of the park's nine lakes, features a rustic bridge and a boathouse where visitors can rent pedal-boats and circle around scenic Strawberry Hill.

The park's massive Victorian greenhouse, called the Conservatory of Flowers, holds the record as North America's oldest existing public conservatory and is a registered national landmark. Other registered historic landmarks here include the 1902 Dutch Windmill, the 1925 Beach Chalet, and the 1888 Francis Scott Key Monument. The park also contains a sizable collection of statuary scattered throughout its rolling hills and intimate enclosures.

In addition to natural beauty and historic landmarks, the park is home to cultural venues and sporting attractions. The Music Concourse, the Japanese Tea Garden, and the first M. H. de Young Memorial Museum building are remnants from the successful 1894 California Midwinter International Exposition, San Francisco's first World's Fair. Sports venues on the grounds include baseball diamonds, soccer fields, tennis courts, a golf course, and the newly remodeled Kezar Stadium. On Sundays and holidays, a stretch of John F. Kennedy Drive is closed off to vehicular traffic, allowing skaters and cyclists free reign of the wide avenue.

# Conservatory of Flowers

As North America's oldest existing public conservatory, San Francisco's Conservatory of Flowers is the crown jewel of Golden Gate Park. Thanks to continuous preservation efforts over the decades, this humid tropical sanctuary has been welcoming visitors into another world of exotic orchids, palms, carnivorous plants, and numerous other species of tropical flora for over 125 years.

The elegant Victorian conservatory was commissioned by real estate magnate and philanthropist James Lick and designed by greenhouse manufacturers Lord and Burnham of Irvington, New York, who modeled it after the conservatory in the Royal Botanical Gardens of Kew, England. The 15,000-square-foot building was shipped in segments from New York by sea to the San Jose-based millionaire, who kept it in storage until his death in 1876. Several prominent businessmen purchased the conservatory from the Lick estate the following year and presented it as a gift to the San Francisco Park Commission. In 1879, the erection of the conservatory was completed and it opened to the public as Golden Gate Park's first structure and as California's first municipal greenhouse.

Four years later, a boiler exploded and destroyed the main dome, but local banker Charles Crocker donated funds for its restoration that same year. The dome was damaged by fire again in 1918, and structural instability caused the closing of the conservatory in 1933. After repairs, repainting, and reglazing, the building was again opened to the public in 1946. A severe windstorm in 1995 caused the closing of the site for eight years while a major three-phase restoration of the landmark was undertaken. The conservatory's grand reopening was in September 2003.

## Japanese Tea Garden

Although it was originally designed as a humble temporary exhibit for the city's 1894 World's Fair, this one-acre garden became a permanent fixture in the park. Park superintendent John McLaren entrusted the garden's care and development to Makoto Hagiwara, a Japanese-American aristocrat who created the original fair exhibit. Under Hagiwara's care, the garden soon grew to encompass nearly five acres of manicured gardens, bridges, and ponds, and acquired a tea house.

In the teahouse visitors can sip tea and have a fortune cookie. Hagiwara is credited with introducing the fortune cookie to the United States. The renowned confection is mistakenly thought to be of Chinese origin; it is, however, actually Japanese. Hagiwara gave his sweetened American version of the Japanese New Year's cracker out to Tea Garden visitors beginning in the early 1900s. In 1915, he formally exhibited the confection at the Panama-Pacific International Exposition in San Francisco.

# Stern Grove

This park was given as a gift to the city of San Francisco in 1931 by Rosalie M. Stern, philanthropist and former president of the San Francisco Recreation Commission, in memory of her late husband, businessman and civic leader Sigmund Stern. The grove was originally owned by the George Green family, who adorned the site with eucalyptus trees and built there the popular Trocadero Inn, a recreation spot in operation until 1916. Redwood and fir trees were later added around the park perimeter, creating a type of natural amphitheater with excellent acoustic properties.

In 1932, the grove officially opened as a public park and, two weeks later, hosted the first of hundreds of open-air San Francisco Symphony concerts to be held in the grove over the decades.

Mrs. Stern organized the Stern Grove Festival Association in 1938, a nonprofit organization mandated with providing seasonal music concerts and cultural events that are both accessible and free to the general public. Religious, political, or commercial use of the grove is strictly prohibited by the association's charter. The popular Midsummer Music Festivals began that same year, and have continued as a local tradition to the present day, bringing open-air music, dance, and theatrical productions to anyone and everyone free of charge. Mrs. Stern chaired the Stern Grove Festival Association until her death in 1969, was succeeded by her daughter Rhonda Haas Goldman until 1996, then by her grandson Dr. Douglas E. Goldman, who currently serves as Festival Chairman.

## San Francisco Botanical Gardens at Strybing Arboretum

Strybing Arboretum is named after Helene Strybing, who donated the funds to create the lush arboretum in Golden Gate Park, complete with 55 acres of botanical gardens featuring over 8,000 different varieties of trees and plants from around the world. Three climate-specific grand gardens feature Mediterranean, temperate/mild temperate, and tropical plant varieties. Smaller specialty gardens spread throughout the arboretum include the Biblical Garden, Garden of Fragrance, Rock Garden, Takamine Gardens, James Nobel Dwarf Conifer Garden, New World Cloud Forest, Redwood Nature Trail, Eric Walther Succulent Garden, Heidelberg Hill and Magnolias, Old World Cloud Forest, Jennie B. Zellerbach Garden of Perennials, Primitive Plant Garden, California Native Plants Garden, and other geographically distinct gardens featuring specimens from South Africa, Mexico, Australia, New Zealand, and Chile.

The park houses a bookstore and a reference library that contains roughly 18,000 volumes of botanical works. The library's garden terrace is landscaped using limestone blocks that were once part of a medieval monastery complex in Spain. Publishing magnate William Randolph Hearst purchased the Monastery of Santa María de Oliva in the early 1930s. With plans for its reconstruction at Wyntoon, his vast northern California estate, he had the entire complex dismantled and shipped to San Francisco. As the Depression Era put a stranglehold on Hearst's pocketbook, his original plans were scrapped, and he instead sold the historic stones to the city of San Francisco for $25,000. Since 1941, the crates of meticulously numbered and catalogued stones have been stored behind the M. H. de Young Memorial Museum. Two fires in 1959 burned off some of the reference numbers, rendering the historic abbey little more than a massive jigsaw puzzle with little chance of ever being reconstructed. A small Trappist monastery near Chico recently acquired nearly half of the historic stones, with which it plans to reconstruct the Spanish monastery's chapter house and refectory at its Abbey of New Clairvaux in Vina, California. Some of the remaining stones have been used around Golden Gate Park, as a retaining wall in the Japanese Tea Garden, pathways in the National AIDS Memorial Grove, and as a fountain, planter bed, and walkway in front of Strybing Arboretum's library.

## Ocean Beach and the Great Highway

Now part of the Golden Gate National Recreation Area, this picturesque beach on the Pacific coast has been an attraction for San Franciscans since 1859. The beach stretches roughly from the Cliff House and Seal Rocks in the north to the San Francisco Zoo and Fort Funston in the south, and is bordered by the Great Highway, one of San Francisco's most scenic motor routes. From Lincoln Way to Sloat Boulevard, the Lower Great Highway, an earlier version that lies slightly more inland, runs parallel to the Great Highway and its massive concrete esplanade, which were completed in 1929.

Ocean Beach was once home to a Coney Island-type amusement park known as Playland-at-the-Beach. From the 1930s to the '60s, amusement mogul George K. Whitney and his brother, Leo, owned and operated the popular venue along with other coastal attractions, such as the Cliff House and the Sutro Baths. Poor attendance and structural deterioration of the Sutro Baths and Playland-at-the-Beach during the late 1960s eventually necessitated their demolition.

Today, Ocean Beach is a favorite spot for sunbathing, swimming, fishing, jogging, and cycling. The northern portion of the beach is home to the landmark Cliff House restaurant, the Sutro Baths ruins, Seal Rocks, and a camera obscura. At Fort Funston, the southernmost section of the beach, hand-gliding enthusiasts regularly make their departures and landings from the sandy dunes.

# San Francisco Zoo

Before the turn of the twentieth century, San Franciscans were able to view a limited number of exotic animals in the city, both at Golden Gate Park and at Woodward's Gardens, an amusement resort in the Mission District that was sadly demolished in 1893. In 1929, the Fleishhacker Zoo opened in the southwestern corner of the city at the site of what is now the San Francisco Zoo, and most of the animals from Golden Gate Park were moved there. The zoo's namesake, Herbert Fleishhacker, was a wealthy banker and president of the San Francisco Park Commission who collaborated with George Bistany, the zoo's first director, and architect Lewis P. Hobart to design the majority of the zoo's buildings. The Elephant House, Lion House, Monkey Island, Aviary, Bear Grottos, and Sea Lion Exhibit were all part of the $3.5 million project, which was financed by the Works Progress Administration during the Great Depression.

In the early 1940s, publishing magnate William Randolph Hearst donated several exotic animals from his private zoo on the grounds of his castle in San Simeon, California. At the same time, the name of the zoo was officially changed—at Fleishhacker's request—to the San Francisco Zoological Gardens. In 1954, the San Francisco Zoological Society was formed. For forty years it aided in raising funds, acquiring new animals, and expanding the zoo's facilities until, in 1993, it assumed full management and operations control of the zoo through a lease partnership agreement with the city.

Today, the zoo houses over 250 species of animals, and the majority of exhibits have been either completely rebuilt or restored. Recent additions include the African Savanna, the Lipman Family Lemur Forest, the Feline Conservation Center, the Australian WalkAbout, Puente al Sur ("Bridge to the South"), and the Children's Zoo with Family Farm and Meerkat and Prairie Dog Exhibit. Favorite veteran exhibits include Gorilla World, Koala Crossing, and Penguin Island, as well as the daily (except Monday) Big Cat Feeding in the Lion House. The hand-carved wooden Dentzel Carousel and the Little Puffer miniature steam train, both installed by Fleishhacker in 1925, continue to entertain new generations of zoo visitors today.

*Ring-tailed lemurs.*

*Left: The* Balclutha, *built in 1886 and used to transport coal and whiskey from Britain to San Francisco.*

# San Francisco Maritime National Historical Park

With its Maritime Museum, Library and Research Center, and fleet of historic ships at Hyde Street Pier, it's no surprise that this unique historic park is visited by over half a million people annually. Located at Aquatic Park between the Marina and Fisherman's Wharf, the national historic park has been bringing to life San Francisco's rich maritime history since 1950.

The park is officially run by the National Park Service, but the nonprofit San Francisco Maritime National Park Association (SFMNPA) coordinates quite a lot of the attraction's activities. They offer guided tours of the 1886 square-rigger *Balclutha*, for example, giving visitors the chance to see firsthand the historic vessel's main deck, captain's cabin, and poop deck. The first deck of the 1890 steam ferryboat *Eureka* is also open to visitors. Other historic vessels in the park include the 1891 scow schooner *Alma*, the 1895 schooner *C. A. Thayer*, the 1907 steam tug *Hercules*, the 1914 paddlewheel tug *Eppleton Hall*, and a collection of over 100 traditional small craft. The park also has a visitor's center and maritime gift shop, and the SFMNPA offers educational programs on site, including boat building and woodworking classes.

The *U.S.S. Pampanito*, a restored World War II submarine docked a few blocks east of the park at Fisherman's Wharf's Pier 45, is also run by the SFMNPA as a museum and memorial. The Balao class fleet submarine was built in 1943 at Portsmouth Naval Shipyard in New Hampshire and became a member of the elite force of U.S. submarines that helped turn the tide of World War II in the Pacific. The vessel sank six Japanese ships and damaged four others; in all, it sunk more than 27,000 tons of enemy shipping. The ship is open for public tours year-round.

U.S.S. Pampanito.

# Fort Point National Historic Site

Located at the southern foot of the Golden Gate Bridge, this Civil War Era fort was designated a National Historic Site in 1970, and is today managed by the National Park Service as one of many attractions found within the Golden Gate National Recreation Area.

The fortress was constructed by the U.S. Army Corps of Engineers between 1853 and 1861. It served as the primary defense against hostile naval forces entering the Golden Gate until the late 1880s, when new technology rendered brick fortresses of this type obsolete for defensive purposes. Troops and cannons were removed from the red-brick fort by 1900, but the U.S. Army still used the site for storage and training. In the early 1930s, the fort was used briefly as a base of operations for construction of the Golden Gate Bridge. It returned to a functioning defensive fortification during World War II, when nearly 100 soldiers manned searchlights and rapid-fire cannons as part of defensive operations to prevent enemy submarines from entering the Golden Gate.

The historic site features several interesting attractions, including Civil War Era cannons and an 1864 lighthouse (deactivated in 1934). Also open to visitors are the Officers' Mess Hall, Surgeon's Quarters, Officers' Quarters, and Enlisted Men's Quarters, each containing period furniture and historic artifacts.

# Presidio of San Francisco

Comprising 1,480 acres, this national historic landmark is popular with a very diverse crowd from nature lovers and culture-seekers to military buffs. The site became part of the Golden Gate National Recreation Area in 1994, at which time the National Park Service (NPS) was appointed as its custodian. A cooperative public-private agency called the Presidio Trust has managed the park with the NPS since 1998.

This area's first inhabitants were the Ohlone, a Native American tribe that called the often fog-shrouded hills their home for thousands of years. With the arrival of Spanish soldiers and missionaries in 1776, the area became a military outpost of the Spanish empire, called simply the *presidio*, Spanish for "fort." After 46 years of Spanish occupation, the site was under Mexican military control for 24 years beginning in 1822. In 1848, the United States military took control of the strategic location and remained there for the next 146 years, until it handed the fort and its surroundings over to the park service.

The Presidio contains a wealth of natural beauty, including forests, beaches, and scenic views of the Golden Gate. More than 500 former military buildings, many of historic importance, can be found within the park's vast boundaries. The most popular attraction of historic significance in the Presidio is Fort Point, but the park also features other smaller coastal defense fortifications of interest, as well as a historic airfield and park museum.

*Pershing Square at the* Presidio.

*Above: Main cellblock.*

# Alcatraz Island National Historic Park

Located in the middle of the San Francisco Bay, roughly ten minutes north by ferry from Pier 41 at Fisherman's Wharf, this famed twelve-acre rock is best known historically for its 29-year period as a federal maximum-security prison during the mid-twentieth century. The island became part of the Golden Gate National Recreation Area in 1972, and has since been carefully managed and preserved by the National Park Service (NPS) as a national historic landmark and nature preserve.

Local Native American tribes, such as the Miwok and Ohlone, are considered to have been the island's first visitors. Arriving by small reed boats, they would fish along the rocky coast and feast on birds' eggs, which were to be found in abundance due to the lack of four-footed predators on the island. Alcatraz is completely devoid of the freshwater sources necessitated by land animals, but it has always been a sanctuary for local birds of all types. It is currently home to one of the largest western gull populations on the West Coast.

In 1775, a Spanish warship entered the San Francisco Bay for the first time. Explorer Juan Manuel de Ayala took notice of the large island covered with white pelicans, briefly charted its topographical features, and officially named it *La Isla de Las Alcatraces*, The Island of Pelicans. The island was seldom visited during the Spanish and

Mexican periods of northern Californian history. However, after American naval forces seized California in 1846 and the island became U.S. property, it wasn't long until the American government put it to good use.

Just five years after acquisition, the construction of U.S. military defense fortifications on Alcatraz began, and in 1854, the first lighthouse on the Pacific coast was erected there—a welcome sight to the thousands of ships entering and leaving the Bay during the frantic post-Gold Rush Era. Between the years 1859 and 1907, "Fort Alcatraz" served alongside Fort Point and Fort Mason guarding the San Francisco Bay. In 1892, all three fortifications were deemed technologically obsolete, yet they remained in operation into the early twentieth century. During the American Civil War, nearly 400 U.S. soldiers were stationed at the fortress on Alcatraz. This was also the first time that the island served as a prison, housing Union military defectors, civilian thieves, rapists, and murderers, and also the crew of a Confederate ship. Later arrivals to the prison included Native Americans captured during the Indian Wars and military convicts of the Spanish-American War. The prison was used briefly as a temporary jail for San Francisco's incarcerated after the 1906 earthquake and fire.

When the fort was decommissioned in 1907, the U.S. Military Guard promptly began tearing down the old building to make room for a new prison complex. In 1915, that new facility, "Pacific Branch, U.S. Disciplinary Barracks," officially began operations as another military prison. However, during the Great Depression, when a nationwide increase in crime created a severe shortage of disciplinary facilities, the Federal Bureau of Prisons persuaded the War Department to transfer Alcatraz Island to the Department of Justice. They in turn gave the green light for the modification of the army prison into a federal maximum-high security penitentiary, which opened in 1934.

Over the next three decades, "the Rock" housed a total of 1,545 of America's most deadly

killers and seasoned criminals, including many high-profile gangsters such as Al Capone, George "Machine Gun" Kelly, and Alvin Karpis aka "Public Enemy Number One." Robert Stroud, imprisoned at Alcatraz from 1942 to 1959, was portrayed by Burt Lancaster in the 1962 film *The Birdman of Alcatraz*. Prisoners Frank Morris and the Anglin Brothers also achieved some degree of cinematic notoriety by their dramatic portrayal in the 1979 Clint Eastwood film *Escape from Alcatraz*. They are three of only five prisoners who successfully escaped from the penitentiary without a trace—but all are presumed dead. A total of 36 inmates were involved in various unsuccessful escape attempts over the years: two actually made it off the island but were promptly captured, seven were shot and killed en route, and two were confirmed drowned; the other 25 didn't get far before being tossed back in their cells with extra punishment.

By 1963, the maintenance and operating costs at Alcatraz prompted Attorney General Robert Kennedy to close the prison. In 1969, a large group of Native American political activists occupied the island for 19 months, successfully using the event to further public awareness of Native American

issues in the media. In 1971, federal agents removed the few activists who still remained on the island and began bulldozing some of the buildings. Luckily, the demolition of history stopped when the island received landmark status the following year as part of the creation of the Golden Gate National Recreation Area.

Several historic buildings remain on the island, including a guardhouse and sally port built in 1857, army barracks and apartments built in the 1860s and renovated in 1905, a military chapel and warden's house built in the 1920s, the prison cellhouse built in 1912 and renovated in the early 1930s, and the historic lighthouse from 1852. Every year, millions of tourists take advantage of the NPS's ranger-guided tours of the island and its historic buildings. Nobody lives on Alcatraz anymore, and the island is accessible only by ferry.

# Twin Peaks and Mount Sutro

San Francisco is known as the "City of Hills," and it contains nearly four dozen of them. The highest of these is Mount Davidson at 927 feet. Nearby Twin Peaks consists of two hills, Noe Peak at 922 feet and Eureka Peak at 904 feet, called by Spanish settlers *Los Pechos de la Choca*, "the Breasts of the Indian Maiden." Both peaks are regularly visited by tour buses for their wealth of natural beauty as well as their sweeping views of downtown, the East Bay, and the industrial south city.

Located to the northeast, very close to Twin Peaks, is the 908-foot-tall Mount Sutro, named after Adolph Sutro, a wealthy businessman and mayor of San Francisco from 1894 to 1896. Sutro's heirs owned a mansion on the hilltop, but the entire estate was sold to the American Broadcasting Corporation (ABC) in 1948. A fire destroyed the mansion in the early 1950s, but in 1972, ABC's San Francisco affiliate, KGO-TV 7, joined up with three other local TV stations to build a worthy structure in its place. Perched atop Mount Sutro, the 977-foot-tall Sutro Tower commands an imposing presence and is clearly visible from the Castro and Mission Districts. The three-pronged antenna tower became San Francisco's primary television and radio transmission antenna tower, not to mention its tallest structure, exceeding the height of the Transamerica Pyramid by more than 100 feet.

## Cliff House

At the northwest corner of the city's coastline, the historic Cliff House restaurant offers stunning views of the Pacific Ocean and Seal Rocks. The site also houses a National Park Service visitors' center and historic camera obscura, and ruins of the famed Sutro Baths are nearby.

The Cliff House has gone through three incarnations since its opening in 1863. The first structure was a modest yet elegant luxury hotel, whose guest register boasted the names of well-to-do families such as the Crockers, Hearsts, and

Stanfords, as well as three U.S. presidents. In 1881, the hotel was sold to Comstock mining millionaire and philanthropist Adolph Sutro, who later built a railroad to provide the public with easy access to the hotel, as well as to his Sutro Baths and Museum next door. This first structure was destroyed by fire on Christmas Day of 1894.

Adolph Sutro spent $50,000 rebuilding the Cliff House, which reopened not as a hotel, but as a dining, dancing, and entertainment venue in

1896. The grand, eight-story Victorian building resembled a French chateau and featured a 200-foot-tall observation tower. This splendid architectural gem made it through the 1906 earthquake, but was sadly destroyed by fire a year later.

The current Cliff House restaurant was built in 1909 in a much simpler style than its predecessor—and of fireproof concrete. Ocean Beach amusement park mogul George Whitney bought the site in 1952 from the Sutro family and remodeled the house several times before the National Park Service (NPS) acquired it in 1977. In 2004, the NPS completed a redesign project at Cliff House that retained the 1909 portions of the building, but removed subsequent accretions and added a new north wing. Today, the Cliff House is preserved as part of the Golden Gate Recreation Area, and is a registered San Francisco Historic Landmark.

# Index